PRAISE FOR
SCOOT OVER AND MAKE SOME ROOM

Heather Avis and I have adoption in common. We have a child of another race in common. But most importantly, we have Jesus in common. I love how she uses her voice to spread God's radical message that every single person is made in his image. If you love Jesus, if you want to open your heart and mind to love deeper and be more like him, you will be better for it.

> *Korie Robertson* of *Duck Dynasty* and author of
> *Strong and Kind: Raising Kids of Character*

Heather Avis is a trusted guide, a gifted truth-teller, and the kind of person who makes everyone around her better just by showing up. *Scoot Over and Make Some Room* does all of the same things. In her uniquely endearing way, Heather challenges us to pay attention to the people we are prone to ignore and, in so doing, provides us with a refreshing understanding of what it means to be human. This is the kind of book you can't stop reading but don't want to end.

> *Mandy Arioto,* president and CEO of MOPS International

Scoot Over and Make Some Room is a beautiful reminder of the power of love when it's generously shared with absolutely everybody. Heather Avis and her family are leading us by example. You're going to love this book.

> *Maria Goff,* author of *Love Lives Here*

In a day and age where we hear the loud message, "Go after your dreams, whatever the cost!" Heather Avis reminds us that the road to flourishing is sacrificially loving the least of our sisters and brothers, empathetically listening to the "other," and humbly learning from those who are different from us.

Jessica Honegger, bestselling author of *Imperfect Courage* and founder of Noonday Collection

Heather Avis writes with humor, humility, and honesty about breaking out of her "sweet little bubble" to create a world that makes space for everyone. She refreshingly names injustice and invites readers to learn *with* her, not just *from* her. Be prepared to laugh, cry, and have some of your own behaviors and beliefs challenged.

Kathy Khang, activist, speaker, and author of *Raise Your Voice*

Scoot Over and Make Some Room is a book about radical love—love that paints a vibrant narrative of family, challenging social norms, and harmful constructs while inviting us into an inclusive, more loving world.

Lisa Gungor, coleader of the musical collective Gungor and author of *The Most Beautiful Thing I've Seen*

This book is the best! Heather Avis invites us into a sacred place with honesty and boldness as she proclaims truth about the equality of all people. As she shouts the worth of those who are differently abled, she isn't afraid to say the hard things and lay it all on the table as we make room in our hearts, our vocabulary, our homes, and our friendships for everyone we encounter.

Mica May, founder and CEO of May Designs

Scoot Over and Make Some Room is both memoir and prophetic invitation, woven together with humor and compassionate insight. Heather Avis's writing reminds us that everyone matters and that the world is a more beautiful place when we make room for the people who are often pushed to the margins.

Hillary McBride, therapist, researcher, author, and podcaster

If you've ever wondered how you can make a difference in the world, read this book. Heather Avis leads us with humility, honesty, and simple brilliance to demonstrate what it looks like to live a life of true love. She shows us that the way is simpler than we ever imagined and that it has the power to transform not only our own lives but also the shape of our communities and even the wider world. Don't miss this one.

Allison Fallon, bestselling author and founder of Find Your Voice

Making space for unexpected friendships requires intentionality and a willingness to get uncomfortable. Heather Avis finds the extraordinary in the most ordinary moments of everyday life, encouraging us to lean into challenging situations with an expectation that we'll be transformed in the process. It's when we come alongside and learn from those the world ignores that our hearts expand to love more deeply and justly. This book will warm the spirit and give a swift but gentle kick in the pants so we can all create places not just to live but to belong.

Jenny Yang, vice president of advocacy and policy at World Relief

Also by Heather Avis

The Lucky Few

SCOOT OVER AND MAKE SOME ROOM

Creating a Space
Where Everyone Belongs

HEATHER AVIS

ZONDERVAN®

ZONDERVAN

Scoot Over and Make Some Room
Copyright © 2019 by Heather Avis

Requests for information should be addressed to:
Zondervan, 3900 Sparks Dr. SE, Grand Rapids, Michigan 49546

ISBN 978-0-310-35483-3 (softcover)

ISBN 978-0-310-35485-7 (audio)

ISBN 978-0-310-35484-0 (ebook)

The author is represented by Alive Literary Agency, 7680 Goddard Street, Suite 200, Colorado Springs, Colorado 80920, www.aliveliterary.com.

Cover design: Curt Diepenhorst
Cover photography: Sami Lane
Interior design: Kait Lamphere

Printed in the United States of America

19 20 21 22 23 24 25 26 27 /LSC/ 15 14 13 12 11 10 9 8 7 6 5 4 3 2 1

To my three children—
Macyn Hope, Truly Star, and August Ryker.
I have learned more from the three of you
in the past ten years
about love, forgiveness, bravery,
and what it means to truly be human
than I could have learned
in a lifetime without you.
Being your mom is the gift of my life.

CONTENTS

FOREWORD

I'm so grateful to have a friend like Heather Avis, for a million reasons, but at the top of the list is this: Heather inspires me to love people better—to open my heart wider, to include people who are often overlooked, to learn from people who offend me, to use my voice and my resources to advocate for people who deserve more esteem and love and dignity than our culture generally offers them.

Heather and I met in the international terminal of the Newark airport, late at night, in the middle of a blizzard. She was a friend of a friend, a last-minute addition to an international trip my mom and I had planned. Newark was the meeting point before a long flight to Tel Aviv, and the handful of us who made it there without issue now sat around a table trying to figure out what to do about the rest of our group, scattered and delayed at airports around the country.

The trip was ten days of early mornings, late nights, long bus rides, and complex conversations about politics, history, and religion. Also jet lag.

If you've traveled internationally with a group, you know what happens—you see it all. You see what people are like when they're tired or hungry. You see what people are like when they're uncomfortable with the conversation or the company. You see who gets short with servers when their orders come out wrong and who's always, always late for the bus.

And for ten days I watched Heather treat people with tenderness and dignity. I watched her look for who might be left behind or left out. I watched her ask questions that opened the conversation wider. I watched her build rapport with people she'd just met, learning something about them or developing a little inside joke with them.

It came as no surprise to me, then, to learn that she is an advocate for inclusion. Of course she is. I've watched her do it every time I've been with her, anywhere in the world.

One of my central passions is hospitality, and over the years, I've fallen in love with many different definitions for it. A few favorites: "Hospitality is love with snacks." "Hospitality is giving people a place to be when they would otherwise be alone." "Hospitality is holding sacred space for people to be truly seen and heard." And recently this one: "Hospitality looks around and asks, 'Who's not at this table?' and extends the invitation."

That's what this book is about, and that's what Heather's life and work are about—asking who's not at the table and extending the invitation.

In an increasingly fractious and fractured age, we need the practices of inclusion and invitation so desperately, and Heather Avis leads us into this way of living with so much honesty and grace. I'm so grateful for her friendship and her example in my life, and I'm grateful for this book, because each reader will now have Heather's example in his or her life too.

Shauna Niequist

LET'S GET
STARTED

On my thirty-sixth birthday, I sat at a table in my friend's backyard holding a plastic cup and listening with a humble heart as several of my friends went around the table and toasted me. A theme quickly began to emerge as more than one person stated, "You never have to wonder what Heather is thinking!" and we all laughed out loud.

Without a doubt, speaking my mind is definitely one of my finer qualities, though perhaps to a fault. I quiet down when I'm in a larger group with people I don't know, often waiting to be asked a question or my opinion before I jump into the conversation. But when I'm with my friends or in a larger group of people I know, it's true—you never have to guess what I might be thinking. Some people call it being opinionated. I like to think of it as having strong convictions. My sweet and wise dad says I'm a person who, in biblical terms, provokes others toward love and good deeds (Hebrews 10:24).

"Opinionated," "strong convictions," "provoker," "one who spurs others on"—whatever you want to call it—at this point in my life, I gladly own this aspect of my personality. But it has taken me some years to own it, and a few additional years to refine it—a refining that will no doubt continue for the rest of my life.

In my younger years, this aspect of my personality manifested itself in a know-it-all confidence, though it wasn't long until I lost my swagger. I often tell people I knew everything in my twenties and nothing in my thirties. Case in point, when I got my first job teaching high school at twenty-two, I walked onto that campus ready to show everyone how to be a good teacher. Today, if someone were to offer me a classroom, especially one full of high school students, I'd tiptoe into the room knowing I had more to learn than I had to offer.

When I look back at the path my life has taken, I thank God for creating me to have strong convictions. As I've worked on refining my opinionated self, God knew the road ahead would require me to stand boldly in the convictions of my heart. I am the mother of three children, all of whom are adopted and all of whom find themselves on the fringe of societal norms. Two of my children have Down syndrome and one is a different ethnicity than I am. God knew the advocacy hat I would be required to wear for my children—that it is tall and heavy as heck—and that I would need strong, opinionated, and provocative shoulders to carry the weight of it.

It has taken me years to be able to wear my advocacy hat well. At times, I have been clumsy and foolish as I tried to carry it on my own and without doing the hard work required to strengthen my shoulders and improve my balance and agility. I've learned, and continue to learn, that I gain strong shoulders, improved balance, and agility when I hold my opinions loosely and surround myself with people whose opinions differ from mine. I've learned to shut my mouth, open my ears, and really listen to people I had been prone to tune out. And I've learned to trust my God and my gut when the world around me seems to be spinning out of control.

God knew as I provoked others on toward love and good deeds, I would need them to become listeners as well. If I want the world to see the worth and value of my children, who are so often categorized as "other," I need the world to tune its ear to their voices and choose to listen.

And all of this—listening and trying to be listened to— is really hard work, friends. Listening to the voices of those we have never chosen to hear before can be in-your-face uncomfortable, messy, and sometimes hurtful, and it almost always requires prescription-strength humility pills. It's the kind of work we can easily ignore—and the world, our society, our schools, and our churches often do. It's the kind of work that requires us to die to ourselves—to not only put others first, but to put our very "enemies" before ourselves.

Every day, I step into the noise of this deafening world, demanding that it tune in to the voices of my children and others like them, asking people all around us to scoot over and create a space for my children. To create a space for people who don't look like them, think like them, talk like them, or perhaps even vote like them. Did I mention this is really hard work?

I want you to know all of these things about me and about

this hard work because, well, just as my dearest family and friends don't ever have to wonder what I'm thinking, I don't want you to have to wonder where we are going together with this book. I want to tell you about some of the ways I've had to scoot over for others, and how my kids, because of their different abilities and brown skin, have yet to find an equitable and honoring amount of space in this world. I want to share how important it is for all of us to recognize this, own it, and take action. And in the process of all that, let's just say that, together, we're going to do a lot of scooting!

And here's the thing. The more I reflect on the life of Jesus, the more I see how relentless he was in teaching others to scoot over. Sometimes gently, sometimes forcefully, but always purposefully, he modeled what it looks like to carve out space in the world for those who live on the fringes, the ones for whom society had no interest in making room. He never used his privilege or power to advance himself, but rather devoted his ministry to seeking out the "other" in his society and encouraging his followers to do the same. Whether it was sharing a meal with tax collectors, having physical contact with lepers and others who were considered "unclean," or inviting women to engage in spiritual conversations to which only men had access, Jesus consistently created space for those who spent their lives being pushed aside. With every encounter, Jesus said to those who had taken all the available seats, "There is unlimited space at this table, so scoot the heck over!"

I've learned a lot in the last nine years as a mother of two children with Down syndrome and one child with brown skin, but I have a lot more to learn. That line is worth repeating: *I have a lot more to learn.* But even though the lessons I've learned so far on the topics of motherhood, different abilities, and race are a drop in the bucket, I'm not willing to wait until I know more to do something. My proximity to the "other," as my children are so often regarded, has taught me that standing up for those who are excluded from the privileged majority is not optional or something I can wait to do.

Now is the time to shout the worth of my children with Down syndrome.

Now is the time to shout the worth of my daughter with brown skin.

Now is the time to shout the worth of all who need someone to speak up for them and say to the world, "Scoot the heck over!"

As a passionate advocate who also knows she still has a lot to learn, I sometimes worry that I'll be misunderstood. I am not here to be bossy, and I have no desire to go back to the know-it-all ways of my twenties. I also know that my reality does not invalidate the reality of another. And I recognize the simple truth that I can't know what I don't know. But I never want to use this truth as an excuse to sit comfortably in my ignorance. That's why it's important to me that you know that what I share on these pages are my opinions, my experiences, my convictions, and, above all, my story.

That being said, I believe everyone has a story that needs to be told and should be heard. I believe the power of story has the potential to break down barriers and create a space for people who don't yet have a seat at the table. I believe story *and* relationship together have the power to open our hearts to whomever the "other" might be in our lives, and ultimately to bring about the peace and unity our world is lacking today. We don't have to agree with one another, but we must take time to listen to one another.

I also have a sneaking suspicion that each and every one of us has felt like the "other" at some point in our lives—hoping someone will scoot over, open up a seat at the table, and invite us to share our stories.

This book is full of those kinds of stories. The kind I hope will have you nodding your head and whispering, "Me too!"— because those two words are so powerful in this motherhood journey—and also shaking your head as you think, *I don't totally get it, but I'm willing to listen and learn*. It has been these two postures that have gotten me through my motherhood journey so far. These two postures have helped me realize just how much space I was taking up in this world, and how much scooting over was required of me.

And I want you to know in my deepest heart of hearts that I have a seat for you around my dining room table, a place for you to come and share your story with me. Just a heads-up that there will probably be oatmeal from breakfast cemented on the table and remnants of last night's tacos on the floor. You should also be warned that the kids will interrupt at least one hundred times, and we will most likely have to break at some point for a dance party in the kitchen. But there is room for you here.

As I wrote this book, I prayed for you. I prayed that God would give you the courage to do whatever "scooting over" requires of you right now. I also prayed that others would make room for you, giving you a seat at the table so you can share your story and your life in the spaces where it's needed most. My prayer is that, together, we will have hearts that are tender and eager to see the spaces in our lives where a little scooting over may be required of us.

Chapter 1

TAKE A BREAK
ALREADY

I sat in the oversized booth with my husband, three small children, my parents, and my younger sister, Hana, who, at the time, did not have kids. The restaurant was noisy with the sound of clanking dishes, and rock 'n' roll music was playing just loudly enough in the background that my kids felt the need to shout when speaking. I tried to engage in adult conversation with my sister and parents while simultaneously placing my hands gently on my children's shoulders, shoving them down on their bottoms, and dividing pizza slices and pasta noodles among their plates—even though they seemed incapable of sitting still long enough to eat anything.

"I have a question," said Hana, who had been watching the circus on my side of the booth. "Do you ever feel like you've lost yourself? You know, since having kids?"

Cue tactical defense systems. I registered her question as a backhanded criticism, and I was surprised by my knee-jerk response. "Um, yeah!" I answered, my tone a little too snarky. "How couldn't I?" I raised my eyebrows and gestured toward my needy, wiggly, shouting children as if to say, *Do you see what is going on here? My reality? Of course I've lost myself!*

Then as if on cue, my middle daughter's curly head popped in front of my face as she blurted out, "I need to go potty, Mommy!" which effectively ended the conversation.

After we got home that night, I found myself stewing about my sister's question. There was no denying it—I *had* lost myself since I'd become a mom. Even that night at dinner, I hadn't been able to take two consecutive uninterrupted bites or complete a coherent sentence because of the kids. Not to mention the fact that every morning around 5:30 a.m., I'm awoken by someone other than myself—namely, three little munchkins who expect me to be 100 percent "on" from 5:30 in the morning until bedtime—and then some! True, I could choose to get up at 4:30 in the morning and get some "me time." But I'm not crazy, and 4:30 in the a.m. is still nighttime in my world.

There was a time when my first thoughts of the day were about such things as going for a run, jumping in the shower, what to wear that day, or what to have for breakfast. Once children entered my life, I not only lost my morning routine but also part of myself—the part that loves to savor a slowly sipped cup of coffee while quietly reading or just sitting still. The part of me that would *love, love, love* to enjoy that morning cup in a coffee shop, maybe with a scone or muffin, and possibly bump into a friend.

Now my morning routine includes heating up day-old oatmeal, brushing three sets of tiny teeth, putting tiny clothes on tiny bodies, and rushing said bodies to the door to shove some tiny feet into tiny shoes so I can get the kids to school on time. And as the day goes on, the rushing doesn't stop. I'm constantly looking at the clock to make sure every minute is used wisely. Dishes done, laundry folded, emails answered—all before kids get home from school or wake up from naps. And once the kids are home or up from naps, they want to paint and play chase. Argue and disagree. Make a mess and not clean up. Run around outside and, most of all, be with me.

I have learned what every mother realizes sooner or later—when we choose motherhood, we choose sacrifice. There really is no way around it. By whatever means a woman becomes a mother—whether it's planned or unplanned, something she tries desperately for or something that happens unexpectedly—she is faced with choices to sacrifice herself from the moment a baby is placed in her arms.

When we choose motherhood, we choose sacrifice.

There was a time when I questioned my motherhood, even my womanhood, because of my inability to get pregnant. But it didn't take long for me to see those questions for what they are—complete and total lies. Dear woman who is struggling with infertility right now, do not believe yourself any less a woman or any less a mother because of your body's confusion about how to get a baby growing in there. Our motherhood, our very womanhood, does not exist in the functions of our body. No! This thing called motherhood exists in the functions of our soul, in the depths of our heart. Motherhood is a holy, brave, sacred role, sometimes attached to one's womb but always attached to one's heart and soul.

When we choose to step fully into our motherhood, it's impossible to do so without stepping fully into a life of sacrifice. The moment we embrace our children tightly with both arms, we let go of any conflicting dreams, goals, or pleasures we had our arms around before.

So let's go back to that night at the restaurant with my sister. At the time she asked me if I had lost myself once I had kids, I was still relatively new to the whole motherhood gig. My oldest daughter, Macyn, was only five years old. While I had learned a lot in those five years, there was no question I still had a lot more to learn. In defense of my snarky response, it should also be noted that having three children under age five is one of the most stressful and all-consuming seasons in one's motherhood. (Can I get an "amen!" from all the mamas of multiple children under the age of five?) And in all honesty, because I'm a recovering know-it-all—or more delicately put, a woman with strong convictions—it felt as though Hana was criticizing the ways I had chosen to do life, and so my response was defensive.

During the earliest season of my motherhood, one of my strongest convictions was that a mother's most important role is to sacrifice for her children. At the time, that conviction looked like just one thing: *make every sacrifice needed to be a full-time, stay-at-home mom.* I remember telling my husband, Josh, "If we need to move back in with my parents or live in a single-bedroom shack, we will do whatever it takes for me to stay home full-time with the kids."

My parents had made great sacrifices of their own so my

mom could be home full-time with my sisters and me. I felt a strong conviction about doing anything it took to be a stay-at-home mom because that is how I was raised. Josh and I had also struggled for years to become parents. After working so hard to become a mom, the idea of not staying home full-time with my daughter felt painful and nearly unendurable. I had also surrounded myself with other like-minded moms. All of my closest mom friends shared my strong conviction about making any necessary sacrifices to be home full-time with their children.

This was still my mind-set the night I sat across the table from my sister in that noisy restaurant. When she asked me if I had lost myself, my answer was snarky because it was motivated in part by a certain kind of pride. I may as well have said, "Yes! *Of course* I've lost myself since becoming a mom, because the best way to be a mom is to completely lose myself."

Here's the thing though. Now that some time has passed and I'm older and wiser (although I *am* still very young!), my life and my thinking have shifted, allowing me to make room for *other* ideas, *other* approaches, and *other* convictions about motherhood. I am learning to listen, not just to people who are like me, but to people who are very different from me. I want to expand my view of the world and my understanding of God by immersing myself in as many diverse settings as I can and by making space in my life for people who don't look, think, or act like me. And this way of living life—this desire to make room for all the *others*—has shifted my convictions on what it means to sacrifice as a mother.

This shift in how I view motherhood began when my children were five, three, and one and my husband had just accepted a new job in a new city. This meant we had to pick up and start over. I was excited for what God was doing in our lives and for the possibilities awaiting us in this new city, but I was heartbroken to leave behind a community in which I was deeply invested. I was part of a close-knit group of moms, all of whom stayed home full-time, all of whom had been there when we welcomed each child into our family, all of whom had prayed us through both Macyn's and August's open-heart surgeries and what felt like an unending gauntlet of doctor visits. These were women I could call at two in the morning to ask for prayer and medical advice when a child was burning up and puking, women who would drop everything to meet me for coffee and let me cry about how difficult this whole motherhood gig can be. They were more than friends; they were extended family. Leaving them crushed me.

Having people in my home with their feet under my table is one of my greatest loves. So, when we moved, finding and building community was at the top of my to-do list. My husband's new job was at a church, and church people are some of the warmest I know. While all relationship building takes intentionality and time, it didn't take us long to make friends and begin to build our new community.

This new group of friends was different from my previous group. For our first year together, one in which we were just getting to know one another, I was the only one with kids, and the only woman in the group who stayed home full-time. While I missed having middle-of-the-day hangout time with moms and their kids, this new group of friends reminded me of how adults without kids have a lot more freedom to go out and do fun things. Friends without kids are not trapped in their homes at 7:30 every night. Friends without kids are a blast!

Shortly after our move, my new friend Katie invited me to go with her to an evening event in downtown Los Angeles, about a thirty-minute drive from our home in Monrovia. Josh volunteered to stay home with our sleeping babes so I could hang out with Katie and do adult things after 7:30 at night.

To avoid the hassles of traffic and parking downtown, we decided to ride the Metro. Once we got settled in our seats, Katie asked me how my day was, and I told her about everything that had happened with the kids that day.

"What about you?" I asked Katie as I wrapped up what could easily have become a never-ending, one-sided conversation about my three munchkins. "Do you want kids?"

"I definitely want kids," she said. "Just not anytime soon."

"Do you think you'll keep working once you have kids?" I asked. "Or will you stay home?" I asked the questions, but I assumed I knew the answers.

"Oh, I will for sure keep working," Katie said.

"Really?" I said, not even trying to hide my surprise. Katie is a pastor at our church, and I thought, *Surely a pastor knows that being a mom requires the sacrifice of staying home.* But Katie didn't seem to notice the shock in my response.

"Oh yeah, for sure," she continued. "My mom worked while I was growing up, and it was great."

Our train lurched to a stop, ending the conversation. Rather than bring it up again, I decided to sit with it for a while.

Katie's perspective was new to me. I had spent so much time with moms who thought the way I thought that I just assumed it was the way pretty much everyone thought. And to be honest, in many church settings, it's simply the expectation that a mom will stay home full-time to raise her kids.

After several months of living in our new community, I realized that the majority of women I met were mothers who had either chosen to work outside the home or were planning on doing so once they had kids. And everyone's situation was different. I knew of families who needed two incomes to pay the bills, as well as moms who didn't need a penny of the money they made but preferred working to being home full-time with their kids.

As I spent time with these women and their families, I quietly observed and tried to understand how a mom could choose anything other than staying home to raise her kids. I could definitely understand how a mom would have a strong desire to go back to work. When all three of my kids were home with me, I sometimes felt a bit wacky. Okay, *daily* I felt a bit wacky. There were many days I wanted to do anything but be in charge of my needy and helpless little crew. And there were times when the thought of dropping off my kids at day care or leaving them with a nanny was very appealing. But my conviction to be home with my kids always remained the strongest. And yet the more I got to know these women and watch them mother their kids, the more I realized they had so much to teach me about being a good mom.

These moms chose to go to work, and yet they were still really amazing moms. Watching them showed me that motherhood and our ability to mother are not defined by whether we choose to stay home full-time or we choose to work. It also hit home that the decision to work or stay home is not a choice all women have the luxury of making. In fact, it's not an option for most working-class women.

Over the years, as I diversified the kinds of mothers I spent time with, I came to the conclusion that I was wrong in my thinking. I was not wrong for choosing to be a stay-at-home mom. This was and still is my choice because it's what's best for my family and me. But as much as I once thought otherwise, the truth is that the choice to stay home or not is not what defines our motherhood; our motherhood is defined by our choice to step into it fully, no matter what that looks like.

We step into our motherhood fully when we step out of our homes and into the workplace. We step into our motherhood fully when we hand our children over to a babysitter, grandparent, nanny, or day care worker. We step into our motherhood fully when we make sacrifices to stay home full-time. We step into our motherhood fully when we do what is best for us

> Our motherhood is defined by our choice to step into it fully, no matter what that looks like.

and for our families. As I've learned from my working-mom friends, I can see clearly how choosing to work rather than stay home full-time offers so many women what they need to be their very best as a mom.

My working-mom friends have not only shown me how motherhood can take on many different forms, but they've also taught me how to choose myself—to step away from the mom role from time to time. They've shown me that I can be a good mom and still have dinner with my girlfriends, go yard sale hunting on Saturday morning, or spend some time alone at a coffee shop in the middle of the day.

Even so, it took me years to accept that choosing myself was okay. I spent so much time thinking my job as a mom was to choose my kids—to sacrifice myself and my own space in this world—that I was convinced I would only be a good mom if I sacrificed everything for my kids. And by the end of most days, this left me feeling lost and exhausted. The truth is, I wasn't always a great mom when I felt lost and exhausted. I've learned I have to make time and space for myself in order to make space for others, including my children. Which means I must make space in my life for rest—time to step away from day-to-day demands and stresses so I can reflect, refuel, and reconnect with God.

This idea of rest often gets confused with self-care. When I hear women talking about self-care or encouraging others to participate in self-care, it usually entails some form of beauty treatment, eating out paired with retail therapy, or a getaway in which a woman removes herself from her daily responsibilities to relax and unwind.

I have to be totally honest and admit I don't like the idea of self-care, at least not the way the term is thrown around these days, mainly because it strikes me as a very privileged idea. And anything linked to privilege, by definition, means whole people groups are left out. As a mama raising kids who too often find themselves in the left-out group, I've learned to pause and look deeper when something works only for a privileged few and then to ask if I should, or even want to, participate.

Self-care, at least the way our Western culture tends to think of it, may sound like something all mothers have access to, but this simply is not the case. Self-care works for mamas who have means—moms like me, who have a supportive spouse, a community of supportive people, and money to spend on nonessentials. The majority of us who can get our hands on this book and make time to read it likely fall into this category. We have certain advantages. When we sit in our seats of advantage for too long, it's easy to forget that the majority of the world's moms do not have access to the same self-care luxuries we do. In fact, the majority of the world's moms spend every waking moment of their lives making sure their children have enough to eat. Even the very idea of self-care is a luxury.

Whoa! Yup, I went there. It's harsh, I know. And now you may be thinking about putting this book down and never picking it up again. But let's talk about this a little more. I don't bring this up to make a mama feel bad about the bimonthly manicure she gets as an act of self-care. I bring it up because we share a globe with all of the mamas of the world, each one an image bearer of God. The more global our perspective, the more prone we are to be healthy and whole—and to raise kids who have a global perspective and are healthy and whole. Having a global perspective helps us look beyond ourselves.

If you're like me, it's unlikely there are moms nearby who spend every day of their lives trying to keep their children from starvation. But I bet where you live there is a single mom. Or a mom who is a full-time caregiver for a medically fragile child or family member. Or a mom working two jobs because she is the sole breadwinner for the home.

Maybe you are that mom, and every time someone encourages you to "take some time to take care of yourself" or asks, "What are you doing for self-care?" a knot forms in your stomach because you simply do not have time for self-care—and you may even feel resentful toward those who do or those who don't understand why it's not an option for you.

In fact, the very idea of self-care may feel like another "to do" on the never-ending to-do list every mom has tucked into her back pocket. In addition, when we finally get to the "self-care" item on our to-do list, the amount of orchestrating that needs to take place for the kids to be cared for while we care for ourselves adds at least a dozen more to-dos to the list.

When Macyn first came home, I was consumed with all things motherhood and a medically fragile child, and I truly believed the best way to care for her was to completely die to myself and my needs. It was only years later, with three kids in my care, and a lot more crazy in my day, that I began to see the importance of choosing myself by choosing rest. When I actually did take a break from my job as a mom, I discovered my kids were just fine under someone else's care. I also discovered that what I needed most was neither self-care nor total sacrifice—the thing I needed was rest.

The form that rest takes will look different for each of us, but all of us have to first make space for it in our lives. Although rest is ordained by God, who created the Sabbath, I know it doesn't come easy for many of us, which is why we have to *make* it happen. But here's the thing. Rest is about more than stepping away from the kids to get our nails done or spend a day at the spa. Rest is a posture of the heart.

Allow me to repeat that.

Rest is a posture of the heart.

Rest is not about doing what we want when we want to because we deserve it, but about recognizing our need for a God-ordained pause. A pause that requires us to step away from our hands-on job as a mom long enough to reconnect with the heart of God—which in turn helps us be a better mom, wife, friend, and human being. And that's why I feel twitchy about what our culture considers self-care. Self-care connects us to our self, not to the heart of God.

So, what's the difference between self-care and rest? *Self-care* is getting the manicure because you feel you've earned it and you desperately need a break from the kids. Rest is getting the manicure because you recognize the distance that has developed between you, God, the kids, or others, and you need to step away long enough to catch your breath, reflect, and pray. Do you see the different postures of the heart in these two scenarios?

When we take the time to rest, whether relaxing at the spa, going for a walk, eating dinner with friends, or sitting in silence for five minutes (because let's be real, mamas, some days that is all we've got!), we can more clearly see God's love for us—which leads to a clearer picture of God's love for all of humanity, helping us love others in return. I believe authentic self-care looks like rest, and this makes me feel less twitchy because when we stop confusing rest with self-care and see it instead as a posture of the heart, we find that rest is something that's not just for the advantaged but is available for all the mamas in the world.

As we navigate this life and as we raise our kids, I believe our own personal health, as well as the health of humanity, is dependent on our ability to see the space we are taking up in the world, and then to scoot over and make more space for those who don't yet have a seat at the table. But how can we see the space we are taking up in the world if we don't step back and rest long enough for this truth to come into focus?

If I could go back in time to that noisy restaurant, I think I'd have a different response to my sister's question, "Do you ever feel like you've lost yourself? You know, since having kids?" I hope I'd say something healthier, something like, "I used to think that motherhood meant losing myself, but now I think it's more about finding myself in the very best ways."

I am so thankful for all I've learned from both my stay-at-home mama friends and my working-mama friends. For the ways in which they have taught me how I can't make room for others until I'm able to make room for myself. The tricky part of actually implementing this rest thing is that our work as mamas is never done. I have yet to hear a mama say at the end of the day, "Well, everything is checked off my list. I have nothing left to do!" This never happens because it is, in fact, a trick list—as soon as you check off the last item, ten more appear. The list of ways in which we can give of ourselves for our children is never-ending.

So, dear mom friends, go ahead and put "take a break" at the tippy top of your to-do list. For your own health, for the health of your children, and for the health of our world, it is time for you to find—or perhaps more accurately, to *create*—a space for rest.

Chapter 2

NEVER PASS UP AN OPPORTUNITY TO PEE

Pee is a major character in our life story. In fact, let's call him Mr. Pee.

There may have been a time in my life when it bothered me to have pee on my hands or my clothes or my floors or my furniture or my bedding. I'm pretty sure of it. But I can tell you that is definitely no longer the case. Lord, have mercy on a potty-training mama!

Here is how the despised Mr. Pee managed to barge into our lives in just the past twenty-four hours. My youngest child, August, who is four and has Down syndrome, is mostly potty-trained—*mostly* being a loose and relative term. He manages to stay dry most days and nights, but he does not voluntarily take himself to the bathroom—we have to remember to do that for him.

He also recently decided he wants to pee standing up. *Great!* While I have zero experience in peeing like a male, I am with-it enough to know my son will someday pee standing up, so we may as well start now. The problem is, he's not very skilled at it. This brings us back to the past twenty-four hours. I woke up and scooped my son out of his bed, and together we headed to the bathroom. Just as I began to place him on the small green potty chair in the corner of our bathroom, he stiffened up his body and said, "No! I pee big potty. Standing up."

He is too small to reach the big potty on his own, so I stood him up on the rim of the toilet bowl, and he began to pee before I had positioned him for accuracy. And, you guessed it, the majority of the pee did not make it into the toilet bowl. August is my only son, but I have friends who have sons of all ages, and I've heard this is something many males never outgrow!

I cleaned up the pee as best I could, no doubt missing a far-flung splash or two that would just have to dry on its own. I probably could have been more thorough, but who has time for that, right?

When I picked up August from preschool just before lunch, I noticed he had on different pants. In his backpack, wrapped up like a gift in a plastic grocery bag, were his pee-soaked undies and pants.

We managed to get through the next couple of hours with no major potty issues before walking to his sister Macyn's school to pick her up. Macyn is nine and in third grade. When we got there, I noticed she too was wearing different pants. *Oy vey!* Macyn has Down syndrome and spends the majority of her day in a general education classroom with the support of a one-on-one instructional assistant.

"Macyn!" I cheered as she ran toward me and gave me a big hug. "How was your day, babe?"

"Good. I peed my pants," she announced matter-of-factly.

Ya don't say, I thought, but managed to keep my sass to myself. "That is totally okay, Mace," I said. "Lots of people have accidents." It was then that her instructional assistant told me she hadn't even tried to make it to the bathroom. She just sat at her desk and peed a ton of pee (which is actually something I've been tempted to do on occasion, especially during a long movie). Well, it wasn't the first time and wouldn't be the last. Carry on.

We got home, and the next few hours were uneventful, at least where Mr. Pee is concerned. Then just as I was about to start making dinner, I looked at August and discovered his camouflage sweatpants were soaking wet.

"August, did you pee in your pants?"

"Yes."

"Buddy! Why?" The question was rhetorical, of course.

"Because I want to!"

I walked him to the bathroom, and get this, when I pulled off his sweatpants, not only were they wet, but there was a little handful of rabbit-style turds being kept from falling out of his pant leg by the elastic on the bottom of the sweatpants.

"August! No!" At this point I was done. I held his little chin in my hand and said, "August, look in my eyes. Where are you supposed to poop?"

He looked right back at me and said, "I poop in the potty."

"Then *do it!*"

I took a deep breath and began to run a bath.

Side note: Allow me to be totally honest and tell you if he had only peed his pants, I would not have given him a bath. Pee is sterile, right? I think I learned that from an episode of *House.* Anyway . . .

After the bath, Mr. Pee was gracious enough to leave us alone through dinnertime and bedtime. Then, at approximately 1:34 in the morning, I was awoken by the sound of a slamming door. I reluctantly got out of bed and walked across the dark house to see what was going on. My middle daughter, Truly, was on the pot, thankfully making sure to pee in the toilet. Since I was up, I decided to go check on the other two kiddos. I pulled up Macyn's covers and tucked them in around her. Then I leaned over August's crib and noticed his blue sheet was a darker shade of blue right where he was lying. I felt the dark spot, and yup, you guessed it, he had wet the bed.

Dang it!

This was not the first time this had happened, so I knew the best way to go about cleaning up the situation without disrupting August's sleep too much, which included gentle lifting, gentle changing, gentle wiping down. While he sat naked on his little green potty chair in the bathroom, I grabbed a set of clean sheets from the linen cupboard and put them on his bed, grabbed clean undies and pajamas from his dresser, ran back into the bathroom where my naked kid was still sitting on the green potty chair, put on his dry pajamas, and then placed him back in his crib. Like a pro!

In the morning, everyone woke up nice and dry—well,

almost. Macyn still sleeps in Pull-Ups at night, but this is a whole nother story! At least all the bedding and beds were dry, making my life easier.

While the girls ran around getting ready for school, August sat on the kitchen counter and "helped" me make scrambled eggs. As I reached for one of the eggs he was handing me, I noticed he was extra wiggly.

"August! Are you peeing right now?"

His blank stare and the small puddle on the kitchen counter were all the answer I needed.

After cleaning him up and wiping up the pee on the kitchen counter (so gross!), I threw his wet clothes into the washing machine, along with the pile of pee-wet clothes from the previous twenty-four hours I hadn't yet had time to wash.

And then, I kid you not, Macyn had two more accidents that day! The best part, after all of our encounters with Mr. Pee in the previous twenty-four hours, was when my middle daughter, Truly, walked out of the bathroom toward the laundry room with a grimacing look on her face, holding the corner of a pair of her sister's wet pants and undies, followed by a pantless Macyn.

And I thought, *Oh, gosh, our life is a family affair, in all of the ways!*

All of which is to say, these days I pretty much think of pee almost like water. I mean, I clean it up as best I can, but if a little drop gets on my clothes, ehh, no big deal. A few weeks ago, when August took a nap in our Cal-King bed, I discovered he was wet when he woke up. Right in the center of the bed, there was a small wet spot, maybe the size of a paper plate. It was damp more than it was wet, and you know what I did? I left it there! *Well, neither of us sleeps in the center of the bed*, I reasoned, *so no big deal.*

When we first made the decision to adopt Macyn, I scoured the internet for any information I could find about Down syndrome. This was before social media existed in the form it does today, so there wasn't much information out there. When I found a couple of YouTube videos of little girls with Down syndrome dancing, I felt excitement and hope for the daughter we would soon bring home. But what I remember most from my internet research was reading about the trials of potty-training. One article said that kids with Down syndrome often start kindergarten in diapers. That tidbit stuck with me and set my expectations for Macyn and potty-training very low. Even so, I said to myself out loud, "My kid will not be wearing a diaper to kindergarten." And she didn't. But Lord, have mercy, it was still an uphill battle—one that left me scarred and with a little bit of potty-training PTSD.

Macyn's potty-training journey has been a long, long, long, long one. It took her a full eight months to finally "get it." Eight long, pee-soaked months for something to click and for her to start taking ownership of her toilet needs. By then, I was a potty-training mess. Way too obsessed with constantly checking to see if she was dry, making her go pee in the potty, and feeling defeated every time she had an accident, which was at least once a day—for eight months.

Thankfully, when it comes to potty accidents, I've mellowed out—a lot. One of the beautiful things about motherhood is how it stretches and strengthens us. Six years after that eight-month potty-training adventure, I still sometimes pick up Macyn from school and find her in a different set of clothes than the ones she left the house in. But I'm different now. I've scooted. I've learned not only how to make space for my kids to grow in ways they need to, but also how to make space for me to grow as a mom in ways I need to.

For me, potty-training a child with Down syndrome has been about so much more than potty-training. Potty-training my children with Down syndrome has taught me to scoot over and make room for motherhood to unfold in unexpected ways. To not let my unmet potty-training expectations consume me, but rather to embrace the fact that our journey to dry undies will unfold in a different way and on a different timeline. Whenever I make room for motherhood to be what I don't expect it to be, I allow myself the gentleness I crave to become a better mother.

In his book *Ragamuffin Gospel*, Brennan Manning writes, "Gentleness toward ourselves constitutes the core of our gentleness with others . . . The way of gentleness brings healing to ourselves and gentleness toward ourselves brings healing to others."[1] It may sound silly to relate this quote to potty-training, but for all those pee-drenched months, the thing I lacked the most was gentleness for myself—which only made it more difficult for me to be gentle with Macyn, especially when weeks of potty accidents turned into months of potty accidents. Instead, I was frustrated and felt like I was failing—like *we* were failing—when the truth is that where and when my child goes to the bathroom has nothing to do with my success or failure as a parent.

I can laugh now when I share the story of August peeing his pants on the kitchen counter, not just because I've (mostly) overcome my aversion to pee, but because I have learned to be gentle with myself when my kids or I fail to meet certain expectations or somehow break with other social norms. Over the years, and yes, through potty-training, I have been able to scoot over—to get out of my own way enough—to make room for the mother I did not expect to be.

> *I have been able to scoot over—to get out of my own way enough—to make room for the mother I did not expect to be.*

I never imagined that for nine years I would have to make space in my purse for a change of clothes every time I left the house with my daughter. Or that I'd have to make space in her school backpack for an extra pair of clean undies and pants. Or that I'd have to make space in my schedule to pull over when she announced she had to pee. It didn't matter if we were on the freeway or in the middle of an Iowa cornfield, once she made that announcement, we had very little time to find a toilet. Which meant I also made space for a bright green portable toilet seat in my car (and it is still very much in use to this day). We have also disposed of pee on many a freeway shoulder, doing our part to water the weeds in drought-stricken Southern California.

When it comes to potty-training, a lot of parents advocate the "wait until your child is ready" approach, which is sound advice. However, there's a fair amount of otherwise sound parenting advice that only sort of works or doesn't work at all when it comes to kids with different abilities—in our case, kids with Down syndrome. I honestly think if we had waited until Macyn was "ready," she'd still be in diapers. But because of the work I've done to make room to become the mother I did not expect to be, I have the gentleness both my kids and I need to not allow something like Macyn being nine and in Pull-Ups at night to have a strong hold on me. The pressure we moms put on ourselves in these "normal" and necessary areas of parenting is taking up the space we need to become the mothers we did not expect we would need to be.

I have spoken with countless moms of children with Down syndrome about potty-training. Moms like me who were determined their child would not start kindergarten in a diaper. Then the first day of school rolls around and the kid is still in a diaper and it's hard to not believe you've both failed. To the moms who feel like failures for whatever the reason, I say, be gentle with yourself so you can make space for things to unfold as they may. You thought sending your five-year-old to school in a diaper was unacceptable, when in fact it's not. When we gently allow ourselves to be the mothers we never expected we would need to be, a beautiful thing happens: we let go of who we expect our kids to be and allow them to become exactly who God intends them to be.

> A beautiful thing happens: we let go of who we expect our kids to be and allow them to become exactly who God intends them to be.

As a new mom, I had very little gentleness for myself, and even for my kids. All that making space for potty-training to unfold in the way it has—well, it has also created the space I needed to become the mom I desire to be. One of these days, Macy will sleep in undies rather than Pull-Ups and wake up dry. Yes, this is something she can and will do. But not today. And that's okay. The truth is, we are all doing the best we can with what we have. We are all just trying to make it through the day with dry undies, in one way or another.

Chapter 3

FIND YOUR PEOPLE

When Macyn first came home, I went from working full-time as an education specialist to being home full-time as a mom. For years, I had hoped and planned to become a full-time, stay-at-home mom, and I loved this new role. But what I hadn't planned on was what my motherhood would require of me.

When I thought about my life as a stay-at-home mom, I pictured myself meeting other stay-at-home moms in the park, my baby wrapped up tight against my chest in a neutral-colored Moby wrap. We'd lay out hip, multicolored blankets from Mexico—the ones we bought on Etsy—and sit around talking about our baby's latest developments and how amazing cloth diapering is. Every time my stay-at-home mom friend would nurse her baby (never with a cover, of course!), I would say something about how important breastfeeding is in hopes of avoiding judgment when I gave my adopted baby a bottle of formula. And then, to compensate for the poison that is formula, I would pull out my homemade baby food and scoop spoonfuls of organic kale and sweet potato—which had been lovingly pureed together with my homemade organic bone broth—into my healthy baby's mouth.

I know this is not every new mother's dream scenario, but it was mine.

Enter Macyn. It was late October 2008 when she came home with us at three months old. And the very next day, my first full day as a mom, I did wrap her up on my chest in a Moby wrap, but it was maroon because I got it as a hand-me-down. And instead of heading to the park to meet up with other stay-at-home mommy friends, Josh and I headed to the hospital to meet with a surgeon to schedule her open-heart surgery.

In the days and months that followed, meetings at the park with other stay-at-home moms did become a regular rhythm in my life, but when my friends and I sat on the Etsy blanket from Mexico, I did it carefully so as not to yank the cannula out of Macyn's nose, and to make space for the oxygen tank the cannula was attached to. When we talked about our babies' latest developments, I always felt a tinge of jealousy or shame, or a mix of both, because my baby was not reaching milestones at the same rate as her peers without Down syndrome. And quite often, Macyn and I missed out on these meetings in the park because our calendar was full of physical therapy, speech therapy, occupational therapy, or doctor appointments.

To be honest, I didn't resent any of it. While my motherhood was unfolding in a way I hadn't expected, I was still head over heels for my girl. I loved her deeply, and I'd go to the moon and back for her. Plus, it was the only kind of motherhood I knew.

Being a full-time, stay-at-home mom can feel lonely and isolating. When life revolves around the mundane routines of making baby food, changing diapers, doing laundry, and putting away tiny plastic toys, it's not hard for new moms to feel a sense of loss. We know we love our baby. We know we are choosing to be home full-time. But we hadn't realized how much of ourselves would need to scoot over in order to make room for our tiny, helpless child.

Plus, everything—tasks, routines, sleep—is new, and constantly having to flex as we figure out our baby and our motherhood can be totally exhausting. Not to mention how freaking tired we already are, and how the child for whom we are sacrificing everything doesn't seem to give a rip because she is a tiny baby and tiny babies are extremely selfish. And needy! As a new, all-consumed mama, we tend to forget we need to be around other new, all-consumed mamas, and we begin to believe the lie that we are alone in our motherhood.

On top of all the challenges every new mama has, I also quickly realized I was the only mom I knew who understood what it was like to raise a child with Down syndrome or a child with medical fragility. Having a child who doesn't quite fit the mold adds a whole nother blanket of isolation and loneliness. And many days it feels as though this blanket is made of wool and is soaking wet.

Not long after we adopted Macyn, I joined an exercise group for new moms at my church. We'd all gather early in the morning in a Sunday school classroom and work out to Billy Blanks Bootcamp videos while our babies chilled in their car seats or on a blanket on the floor. There were times

I rolled in with Macyn and her oxygen tank and overheard a couple of the moms talking about how difficult life had been because their new baby had an ear infection or something wrong with a finger. On the outside, I'd commiserate and say something like, "I'm sorry, that's so hard!" On the inside, I confess I rolled my eyes and resisted the urge to tell them to suck it up as I pointed to the oxygen line in my daughter's nose or the heart surgery scar on her chest. Other times, all the mamas would gather around to ooh and aah over a child who had reached a developmental milestone I knew would take Macyn months longer to reach. On the outside, I was polite and oohed and aahed along with them. On the inside, my heart would break a bit as I thought, *This is just another way Macyn and I don't fit in.*

These first-time, stay-at-home mom friends loved Macyn and loved me. I knew they tried to understand my reality as a mom to a medically fragile child with Down syndrome, but ya can't know what ya don't know. Ya know? And every time a new mom friend pointed out something about her child that would never be true about my child, the heavy, wet wool blanket of loneliness and isolation felt even heavier and wetter.

I definitely needed these mom friends; there was so much we could and did understand about one another. And more importantly, these mom friends and their children needed a Macyn in their life. But as a mama to my Macyn, I needed something more. I needed someone, another mama—one with a Down syndrome gleam in her eye.

One day when Macyn was about four months old, we were at Panera, waiting for my cinnamon crunch bagel with hazelnut cream cheese (one of my greatest stay-at-home mom discoveries), when ahead of us in line I spotted a mama holding a blond-haired baby boy with bright blue almond-shaped eyes and a button nose. I stepped out of line and walked toward them to get a closer look. As soon as I was positive the baby had Down syndrome, I awkwardly pretended to bump into her so I could start a conversation.

"Hi, sweetie," I said, making googly eyes at the blond-haired, blue-eyed boy and speaking loudly enough to get his mama's attention.

"Oh, hi," the mama smiled at me. Then she looked at her son. "Say hi, Alden."

"Oh, what a cute name!" I adjusted Macyn on my hip so she was facing our new friend. "Macyn, say hi to Alden."

Alden's mama looked straight at Macyn. "Oh my gosh, does she have Down syndrome?"

"She does!"

"So does Alden."

I knew this to be true, which is why I had ventured their way in the first place, but I played dumb. "No way! So awesome."

We ended up sharing a booth that morning. The handsome little boy, Alden, and his mom, Marlena, were as dear as two souls could be. At the end of our breakfast, we exchanged numbers. After a couple more chance encounters with other mamas, a small handful of us were gathering from time to time with our almond-eyed, button-nosed babies. And while each of our children with Down syndrome was developing at a different rate and required different kinds of medical care, that extra chromosome had magically found its way into each of our mama hearts, binding us not only to our children, but also to each other.

Macyn and Alden ended up going to the same preschool, and while we now live in different cities and see each other only once a year, it doesn't matter because we are each other's people. In fact, Alden's parents and I are going to do our darndest to make sure our kids fall in love and get married one day. You may think I'm kidding. I'm not.

Now that Macyn is older and social media is what it is, the number of women I know who are mothers of children with Down syndrome is almost more than I can count. Over the years, I've had the great privilege of gathering together with handfuls of these women, mamas whose eyes share the same Down syndrome gleam as mine. I've spent weekends with moms from all over the country whom I would never have met otherwise, and I've developed close-knit friendships with local families whom I would never have spent time with if not for our kids with Down syndrome.

Not only do these mamas know about heart conditions, feeding issues, and potty-training challenges unique to children with Down syndrome, but they also know about the gift and the beauty that is Down syndrome. With these mamas, I don't have to justify or explain the messy and the magic all tangled up in a Down syndrome diagnosis. They understand without explanation. These mamas are safe havens when I feel battered by the storms found in this Down syndrome world. We are deeply connected because we share a deep sense of both understanding and being understood.

It's not just mamas raising babies with Down syndrome

who need to find each other and be in relationship with one another. We are all made to be in relationship with others. Our need to be loved and to love others, to be known and to know others, is woven into the very fabric of our humanity. When God made humans, we were rolled out together because it is not good for us to be alone. This design for community and relationship became most evident to me and most important for me when I became a mom.

We are deeply connected because we share a deep sense of both understanding and being understood.

I needed to find my people, and then I needed to take it a step further. I needed to find *safe* people. People who "get it." People who have the same gleam in their eye. Because I'm raising kids who don't fit into the molds kids are expected to fit into in order to be successful or at least accepted, I don't fit in either. Yes, finding and spending time with my people helped, but it wasn't enough. Although I couldn't have articulated it at the time, the question I needed to ask was this: *What do I have to do in order to find the kind of community a mama to mold-breaker children needs in order to thrive?* Fortunately, the answer to this question found me before I even knew it was a question I needed to ask. Let me explain.

Toward the end of Macyn's second-grade school year, I met with all of the educators who had influence on Macyn and her school days to discuss what her third-grade year would look like. The trouble was, most, if not all, of them disagreed with me about what would make Macyn's third-grade year the best it could be. I spent hours trying to explain why Macyn should spend her whole school day in a classroom with the other third graders instead of in a special education classroom, and I outlined the support system she would need in order for this to take place successfully. The educators who disagreed with me pointed out my daughter's deficits in an effort to convince me that a separate class would, in fact, be best for her.

After leaving one meeting in which I felt particularly beat-up and misunderstood, I put on my running shoes and hit the pavement in hopes of sweating out some of my frustrations. I put in my earbuds, tuned into a podcast, and found myself listening to an interview with Deidra Riggs. Deidra Riggs is both a mold breaker and bridge builder. She's an author and speaker who knows what it's like to be on the front lines as she tries to break the racial molds that bind us.

I listened intently as she began to talk about an idea she called "furlough." It's a term most commonly used in a military setting when a soldier leaves the front lines of battle and returns home for rest and restoration. "Furlough is when you get to leave the place of duty and go home to the people you know," Deidra said, "people who know you and your story and love you anyway."

My worn-out mama heart filled with emotion as she went on to talk about how home is not necessarily a *where*, but rather a *who*—a person or persons with whom you can let down your guard and be restored. That's what it means to be home—it means to be someplace safe. I began to cry.

For years, and especially for those weeks during the end of the school year, I had been on the front lines of battle, shouting the worth of my kids. I knew I was exhausted and I knew the work was hard, but it wasn't until I listened to Deidra's description of furlough that I could wrap words around what I actually needed. I couldn't remember the last time I had intentionally stepped back from the front lines into a safe place. Until this moment, I had never realized my need for furlough.

I cried that day because of all the resistance and negativity I had been perceiving from the educators at Macyn's school, but I also cried because that's when the enormity of it all hit me. Despite all I'd fought for on behalf of my kids, I hadn't fully reckoned with what it would require of me to raise the kinds of children who break molds.

The young woman in her early twenties who was trying to get pregnant and dreamed of having a family never imagined she'd be the mother of three mold-breaking, world-changing children. Children who would require her to break out of the safe, comfortable mold she'd been living in most of her life. Children who would, at times, feel impossible to parent because of the pressures exerted on them to fit into molds they were incapable of fitting into. Children who would require her to step up to the front lines and wage war against systems that would exclude and harm them.

In the beginning, I tried to get back into the molds where I had felt safe and comfortable. As a white person born into a white middle-class California family in the latter part of the twentieth century, I've been able to slip comfortably into most of the molds around me. That meant I had advantages in life—advantages I never really knew I possessed but will always have access to. Then three kids entered my life, and because of circumstances beyond their control—such as adoption, chromosome count, and ethnicity—they live without many of the advantages I once took for granted. While I am able to jump in and out of the molds I fit into so easily, my children are not.

The world prefers people who fit in. There's nothing wrong with fitting in—it's what enables most systems to function well. But here's the problem. Many of these societal systems, such as our schools, workplaces, and even churches, benefit *only* people who fit into the mold. When a child is born with Down syndrome or brown skin, they enter a world in which, so far, the systems disadvantage rather than advantage them. The societal molds that serve the system are not made for them, or, even worse, the system wants to make separate "special" molds for them. Which is what the educators in Macyn's life wanted to do when they judged that she would fit best in a special education classroom. Macyn has Down syndrome, so that's her mold, right? *Wrong!*

My kids are the main reason I shifted from mold fitter to mold breaker. I knew I needed to step up to the front lines to help break the molds of systems that work only for able-bodied, cognitively advanced, light-skinned people like me. *My kids!* By God's grace, I get to learn with and alongside my kids. And rather than raise kids who fit nicely and neatly into the world around them, I get to raise kids who embrace the uniqueness of who God has made them to be, teaching them to avoid all of the molds that pressure them to fit in.

You know our friend Jesus? He was a mold breaker. Throughout his entire ministry, he placed little bombs of radical love in the molds created by the society he was born into and blew up people's ideas about what—and who—mattered most in life.

Jesus blew up all kinds of social norms, especially when it came to caring for the outcasts of society. His friends would be like, "Dude, you can't interact with that person." And Jesus would be like, "Watch me!" Or the religious leaders of the day would say, "Hey, Jesus, you can't heal someone on the day of rest." And then Jesus would look at them and say, "Actually, I can!" And then his radical love was displayed in ways that literally changed the world.

But disrupting the system and blowing up the societal molds of his day came at a great cost for Jesus. He had a lot of haters. *A lot!* People who felt threatened by the way Jesus challenged their mold-making way of life.

Breaking molds is exhausting, daunting, and at times lonely work. I think this is why Jesus so often put himself on furlough, stepping away from the front lines to go "home" by spending time with his Father. Jesus had the Twelve, his people, but there were times when even his closest friends didn't totally get him. He needed to retreat to his safe place, not only to rest, but to be with the ones who knew him best—his Father and the Holy Spirit.

I fight battles on a much smaller scale than Jesus did, but I still find myself feeling exhausted and alone as I try to shout the worth of my kids at a mold-shattering decibel. And the battle goes way beyond the educational systems. Even when we're out in public, I have to be "on," meaning I am hyperaware of where my kids are, what they're doing, saying, not doing, not saying, how others are perceiving them, and how they are perceiving others.

Getting from point A to point B can feel like "mission

impossible" sometimes. Macyn wants to ask everyone we pass what their name is or where they're going or touch their hair, while Truly is literally doing cartwheels through the parking lot or the Target aisle, and August demands something absurd (and slightly adorable) such as, "I want coffee," and then throws a fit because I won't give him any of mine.

Even when we're around people who know and love us, I still feel like I have to be on. *Is Macyn playing with our friend's hair too aggressively? Will our friend comfortably create boundaries, or do I need to chime in? Is Truly going to say something so off-hand or rude that I won't know how to respond? Will our friend feel uncomfortable because of Truly's remarks?* My shoulders tighten at just the thought of each scenario.

It was only when I recognized my need for furlough that I was able to see where "home," that safe place to rest, really was for me. I had to think about the places I can go with my family, or rather the people I can go to with my family, and feel my shoulders relax as I begin to settle into an "off" place—the place where I can let down my guard and find proper rest.

If you're exhausted because you've been on the front lines for too long, you need to do more than find your people; you need to know which ones you can go home to. The list may be very, very short, and many of your people may not be on the list. If so, that's okay. Sometimes we keep our guard up, even if just a tiny bit, around some of our dearest friends. Even Jesus had to carve out time away from some of his dearest friends on earth in order to experience the rest he needed. So don't feel badly about the places or people in which you do *not* find rest and restoration.

On the flip side, maybe you and your children fit easily into the molds and just the thought of being a mold breaker makes you feel the need for your own furlough. Like me, you and your kids may have advantages simply because of the color of your skin or the ways your life fits the socially acceptable molds. If so, I urge you to consider what it might take to reshape those molds.

You don't have to start with complete and utter destruction. Start by inviting someone to join you who maybe never fit in before. It may mean talking with your kids about seeking out the peer at school who has a different ability and inviting him or her for a playdate. Or talking to your child's teachers and principals about what you can do to help make your child's classroom inclusive for all. Or the next time you're out in public and a little girl who may look a little different and have thicker speech comes up to you and asks you your name and wants to play with your hair, shake off your initial discomfort, give her mama a reassuring smile, and engage.

Consider what it would take to make space for others in the social settings you so easily slip in and out of, such as schools, churches, and parks. And just as those of us on the front lines need to ask ourselves where we can go for furlough, ask yourself what you can do so our need for furlough is less necessary.

The truth is, we all need people in our lives who know us, know our stories, and love us anyway. We all need someone who sees and shares that gleam in our eye. Our very well-being depends on it. I've found my safe place in powerful ties with others through motherhood, faith, adoption, Down syndrome, womanhood, or a mixture of all of the above. People both inside and outside of my family. People who feel like home.

Chapter 4

YOU DO YOU

"Comparison is the thief of joy." I read those words sitting on the couch in our nineteen-hundred-square-foot tract home back in 2006. At the time, it was just Josh and me living in a space too big for the two of us. We'd bought the house a couple years prior, thinking we'd fill it up quickly. But after two years of trying to get pregnant, I was in a place of grief, and three of our four bedrooms remained empty.

I was reading Anne Lamott's *Traveling Mercies*, and she had quoted the words often attributed to Theodore Roosevelt. I took a deep and sudden breath when I read these words and then let them sink in, all the way from my head to my gut. "Comparison is the thief of joy," I whispered to myself. As the words settled, I realized it was more than infertility that was stealing my joy. I was deeply jealous of those around me who were having babies. The more I compared my childless life to their gift of motherhood, the more I robbed myself of joy.

As the story goes, we never did get pregnant but rather added to our family through adoption. The sweet little munchkin we had the honor of calling our daughter was our almond-eyed, button-nosed, chromosomally enhanced Macyn Hope. And as I stepped into the world of all things mommy and baby, I quickly became entangled with the thief called comparison in a new and arguably more dangerous way.

Have you ever heard of the book *What to Expect the First Year*?[2] It's the equivalent of a baby bible, especially for a new mom. Most moms I know own at least four copies before their babies are even born. One copy she buys; one is gifted to her; one she gets for a dollar at a thrift store; and one is handed down to her from another mom. On the face of it, the book seems both harmless and helpful. It basically lays out a child's milestones for the first year of life. Curious what your child should be doing at six months? Just turn to the chapter about six-month-olds, and you can find what your baby should be doing—and what she might be doing if she is especially advanced.

Like I said, a seemingly harmless book, except for this fact: *the entire book is based on comparison.* If your child is meeting the milestones the book identifies, then you can breathe a sigh of relief. If your child is exceeding the milestones or "advanced," then you are an exceptional parent and your child is a genius (both of which are most likely only sort of true, if at all!). But what happens if your child looks nothing like the picture of the baby on the cover of the book? What if your child isn't meeting, much less exceeding, the milestones? I'll tell you what happens. For a first-time mom especially, our friend, Comparison, comes and steals away all of her joy. She worries her child is not "normal." She second-guesses all of her parenting. She feels isolated and insecure. All because the book says her daughter should be pulling herself up to stand by now, and she isn't even sitting up on her own.

In her earliest days, Macyn met most of the milestones common for a baby her age. It was around the six-month-old chapter that I began to question if I should continue to refer to this mama-handbook-bible. By the time Macyn was nine months old, she was still not sitting up without support, even after hours of physical therapy every week. For my own health and sanity, I had to put that book away. My daughter with Down syndrome simply did not fit on the pages of a what-to-expect kind of book. Nothing unexpected ever does.

The comparison game is just that—a game. A game has winners and losers. When played with Macyn in mind, the what-to-expect game made me feel as though my baby and I were losers. But the comparison game cuts both ways. If your child is exceeding all of the developmental milestones, then you begin to think you and your baby are winners.

No matter which team you're playing on, the comparison game is always dangerous because while sometimes you may be winning, a time will come when you will be losing. The point here is not winning or losing. The point is that playing the game at all fogs up the truth—that we and our kids are probably doing just fine just the way we are.

When our middle daughter, Truly, came along, she was born neurotypical and able-bodied, and I found myself pulling the *What to Expect the First Year* book off the shelf. Nevertheless, as soon as I glanced at its pages, I invited comparison into the mix once again. It started slowly. First, I noticed how easily Truly reached her expected milestones and how she landed in the "might even be doing" column. I began thinking she was advanced, maybe even gifted (says every parent of a neurotypical kid!). Then I began comparing her to other babies her age. If she hit a milestone before one of my friends' babies, I owned her "success" like a trophy in my heart. One of my best friends at the time had a little girl who was only one week older than Truly, and when Truly took her first steps before my friend's daughter, I felt all kinds of proud. Which feels strange and ugly to admit, because I was more proud that Truly walked first than I was that she walked at all.

I have yet to meet a mom, or at least an honest mom, who does not suffer from the comparison game. We play this game with our kids and with other parents. As I mentioned, when Macyn was a baby, I constantly compared her to her peers. I did this, even though I knew her Down syndrome diagnosis meant her development would be delayed in most areas. I did this, even though I love the fact Macyn has Down syndrome and I don't need or want her to be anything more than *her* very best, not the very best of someone else.

But not all the pressure to play the comparison game comes from within. In fact, when you have a child with Down syndrome, the whole system of care designed to provide support and help is actually based on, you guessed it, comparison. As soon as Macyn entered our home, we were connected with physical therapists, occupational therapists, speech therapists, and early-start teachers. These kind, helpful saints in their fields of expertise entered our home once or twice a week to work with our sweet, tiny Macyn.

The first meeting was always an assessment. The therapist

would pull out her tools, which were often an assortment of ordinary toys. Then she'd pull out an assessment paper and begin taking notes as she tested Macyn on her development. The tests were always based on comparing her development to that of a neurotypical and physically typical baby her age.

Once the assessment ended, the therapist would go over the results with me, pointing out what most babies Macyn's age were doing and what Macyn, by comparison, was not doing. And every few months, the therapist would repeat the assessment, and the gap between what Macyn was doing and what her "typical" peers were doing grew wider. It took me years to recognize that simply by comparing the abilities of my child with Down syndrome to the abilities of children who do not have Down syndrome, it was communicated to me that Macyn was inadequate. She was inadequate because she had Down syndrome.

Please hear me. Not one of our therapists ever saw or treated Macyn as inadequate. They loved her and cheered her on and wanted what was best for her. However, the systems within which they functioned, by their very nature, served only to point out all of Macyn's deficits, which communicated to me that Macyn was not enough just as she was—which meant we were supposed to help her become more like other kids or, rather, less like a kid with Down syndrome.

This unspoken and unacknowledged message that Macyn was not enough crept into how I parented her. When Macyn was around two years old, I got wrapped up in a Facebook group dedicated to helping our children with Down syndrome be more "typical." This was done through extensive medical testing and an intense regimen of vitamins and prescription medications. People in the group talked about how to make our kids with Down syndrome act, talk, and look more "normal." At first, I was intrigued. I knew Macyn lagged behind other kids her age in speech and academics, and I thought how great it would be to give her everything she needed to better meet the marks she was missing.

I started talking to Macyn's pediatrician about what this group called "the protocol." One of the medications in the protocol is Prozac, and getting a prescription would require Macyn to see a neurologist. So our pediatrician obliged and gave me a referral to a pediatric neurologist. This referral sat on my counter at home for weeks, which turned into months. I often looked at it, but there was always something in my gut that told me not to follow through on booking the appointment.

I continued to be in communication with the people in the Facebook group, but there was always something that didn't sit right with me. Every time I shut down my computer, I felt as though Macyn wasn't good enough. Or that I was failing her as a mom if I didn't do the A to Z protocol every day of the week.

I never did set up an appointment with the pediatric neurologist. In fact, it wasn't long until I left the Facebook group altogether. Honestly? At the time, it was mostly laziness on my part. I felt overwhelmed by the commitment required if we put Macyn on this protocol. We were already spending hours a week with therapists and doctors, and I didn't think I had the time or energy required for Macyn to benefit from this protocol. But something good did come out of this experience. I was now more convinced than ever that Macyn was exactly who she was supposed to be—*just as she was*. And I began to shift my perspective on Macyn and on Down syndrome as a whole.

Fast-forward a couple of years. We were now living in a new city, and Macyn was in kindergarten. As soon as we moved, I once again began searching around for those mamas with a Down syndrome gleam in their eye. I was elated when I found a nonprofit group called Club 21. The mission of Club 21 is to provide educational tools and resources that enable individuals with Down syndrome to be fully included, believing society is enriched when they are. When I found their website, I kept saying yes and amen as I scrolled through every page. And I immediately signed up for any and all of the programs that pertained to Macyn and August.

And would you believe it? Even at Club 21, I found myself battling the joy-suck known as comparison. *Whew!* It's one thing to compare your child with Down syndrome to children who do not have Down syndrome. When you play the child with Down syndrome versus the child without Down syndrome comparison game—which is a tempting, foolish, and dangerous game to play—and you lose, you can comfort yourself with statements such as, "Well, my child has Down syndrome, so of course she isn't going to be able to do _____." Once we decided to invest in programs only for kids with Down syndrome, we lost that comforting rationalization. This took the comparison game to a whole new level.

So there we were, showing up to events at the nonprofit, knowing they served our children and our family in significant ways, yet leaving feeling like defeated failures. I know this was never the intention of these events. Quite the opposite, in fact. But when you're raising a child with Down syndrome and doing all the therapy, tutoring, and extra hours of intentional playtime or academics, and the kid with Down syndrome to your right and your left—doing all the same extra work—is accomplishing more than your child, it can steal your joy right out from under you.

For me, comparison has always been a strange tug between my head and my heart. My heart, being able to see more clearly, was constantly speaking truth:

- Macyn is doing her very best. That's all you can ask of her.
- Macyn has made a ton of progress this past year.
- Macyn is a freaking rock-star slice of heaven, just as she is.

But while my heart was doing its best to hold on to truth, my head was working just as hard to get me to play the comparison game:

- Look how well that child with Down syndrome is talking. Where does he go for speech? I need to get Macyn into more hours of speech.
- Wow, that kid is counting to a hundred! I need to get Macyn the same app for her iPad and commit to working with her daily on it.
- Macyn's friend with Down syndrome is reading full paragraphs and writing so well. Macyn isn't even writing her name yet, and she only has a few sight words. I'm failing as a mom.

My problems begin when I choose to listen first to my head and then to my heart.

One particular Saturday, I was sitting in a seminar for parents when I finally saw comparison for what it was. I was taking notes about ways to help our children with Down syndrome tell time, improve their reading comprehension, add numbers, or any one of the million skills we are told they need extra help with, when the woman teaching the session said very casually, "And isn't that the ultimate goal, for our children with Down syndrome to be more like their typical peers?" She continued on with the lesson, but I stopped listening.

Do I really want Macyn and August to be more like their typical peers? The answer began to churn within my soul, and I knew.

No. No, that is not my goal.

Now I had clarity about my goals for my children with Down syndrome. Now I understood why I had been so hesitant all those years ago to put Macyn on a protocol designed to help her be more typical. Now I saw more clearly that my children's Down syndrome diagnosis was not something to fix or change or mold so they could become more like their typical peers.

If Macyn and August were more like their typical peers, it would mean they were like kids without Down syndrome. *No, thank you!* My kids have Down syndrome. Down syndrome should not and does not define them. No, their humanity and all it is made up of defines them. But Down syndrome is a beautiful part of who they are. It plays out in different ways for each of them, but it is an aspect of them I cherish. And I wouldn't trade their extra chromosome for clearer speech or neater handwriting or even more social appropriateness.

I wouldn't trade their Down syndrome for anything in the world. I finally had the clarity I needed to see the true worth and value of my kids with Down syndrome.

I had become so caught up in comparison that I allowed myself to believe my life would be better if only I did or had what others were doing or had. This was never based on any kind of truth, but only on my foggy ideas of how great someone else's life looked. As I journeyed down this motherhood road and into the Down syndrome world and recognized how much I had allowed comparison to steal from me, the fog began to lift.

I wouldn't trade their Down syndrome for anything in the world.

Not only am I now much less likely to play the comparison game; I'm also able to sit on the sidelines cheering on the people I used to compare my life to. And instead of seeing all the ways I think I am doing life better or worse than the mama to my right and my left, I see that we are simply doing life differently. So instead of comparing myself to these mamas, I'm able to shout out, "You do you, girl."

"You do you!" has become my motherhood mantra. But I want to be clear here and let you know I'm not being flippant when I use the phrase, "You do you." For example, when others assume my children with Down syndrome are "less than," I'm not going to give them a nod and say, "You do you." *No!* I am going to do all I can to show these people they are in fact wrong in their thinking. This "you do you" mentality is more of a way to offer grace to ourselves, to our kids, and to one another. Rather than forcing ourselves or our kids to fit into the molds we were never meant to fit into, we can gently usher ourselves into a grace place.

Here's a story of how this played out in a situation with my daughter Truly. When Truly was six, we would occasionally catch her in a lie. Sometimes the lies were harmless, such as telling her friends we had a pet peacock. But other lies were more serious, such as telling her friends at school that we didn't have enough money to buy food and that she was hungry all the time. Yes, this really happened. I learned about this lie from a mom whose daughter was feeling concerned for Truly and asked her mom how they could help. Her mom, knowing our family well enough to know there was no need to worry about us going hungry, called to let me know about Truly's story. *Oy vey!*

As a parent who loves Truly, I don't say to her, "Welp, you're a liar. No problem, girl. You do you!" Of course not. But I also don't look at her and say, "See all those other little six-year-old girls? They're not telling lies. They're telling the truth. You should be more like them." *No way!* Rather, I hold this piece of her with grace. I do my best to teach her the importance of telling the truth, but I also try to create a space for her to receive positive attention for her creativity and imagination. Do I fail at this most days? Yes! Yes, I do. And as I repeatedly fail at being gentle and gracious with Truly, especially with her faults, do I say to myself, *Welp, you lack patience and grace for your kid. No problem, girl, you do you!* Of course not.

Owning and speaking this "you do you" mantra is about recognizing that there is more than one way—or let's be honest, more than one hundred ways—to respond to life. I wish I'd known that truth all those years ago when I was battling infertility.

There were so many ways I compared my life to the lives of women around me who were getting pregnant. I let my joy slip away when I thought about how one friend had been married for only a year when she got pregnant, and how another was struggling financially when she and her husband decided to have a baby.

I thought the fact that Josh and I had been married for a few years and were financially stable made me a more deserving person to have a baby. But the truth was, my friends' choices were just different from my choices. Comparison was trying to make me believe different was bad, when all along I should have been saying to those friends, "You do you!" "You do you" gives us permission to be grateful for who we are and who our kids are. It makes it possible to recognize and celebrate that God has made each of us incomparably unique and supremely beautiful.

So dear mamas, dear women, let's make a commitment right here and now to stop allowing comparison to steal our joy. Instead of playing that comparison game, let's commit to the "you do you" mantra.

You feed your child organic, homemade baby food? *You do you!*

Your child has been eating chicken nuggets and French fries every night for the past ten years? *You do you!*

You don't own a television or any mobile devices? *You do you!*

Each kid in your house has their own iPad and iPhone? *You do you!*

You stay home full-time and care for your kids? *You do you!*

You work full-time and your kids go to day care? *You do you!*

You send your kids to public school and don't give one minute of your time to volunteer for the PTA?

You run the PTA?

You homeschool?

Let's say it all together now, *You do you!*

The reason we parent and live life the way we do is that we believe it is the best way to do it. Let's hold this belief with gentle, grace-filled care, making sure we're not comparing and judging the way someone else does life simply because it's different from the way we do life. And let's not let the ways someone else parents and does life steal our joy.

Let's fully recognize and embrace that our lives and our families and our stories are so uniquely ours that we could never and should never want to be like someone else. And when we see a mama parent her children in a way that is safe and healthy, yet totally different from our own parenting ways, let's be quick to give her a wink as we smile and point to the "You Do You!" button we now wear everywhere we go.

Chapter 5

TRY SPEAKING UP

I want to tell you an embarrassing story, but first I need to give you three pieces of background information.

1. During the years when we brought our kids home, we lived in a classic Southern California four-bedroom, two-and-a-half-bathroom tract home within a Homeowners Association (HOA). Our little four-block community was made up of a hundred homes or so. There were four different models spread out up and down each street, and except for the stucco walls painted different shades of peach and beige, the houses were identical. We had a decent-sized backyard, with a tall wooden fence that marked the perimeter of our property, as well as the properties of the two houses behind us, one to our right and one to our left. Our HOA included a community pool situated in the center of the four blocks of houses.

2. Truly came home when she was six months old. From the time she was a baby up until the present day, she has been an independent go-getter who has plans of her own. This aspect of her personality goes with her wherever she goes. For example,

when she was in first grade, during our first parent-teacher conference, her teacher started out the meeting by saying, "Well, Truly does what Truly wants to do!" It took all kinds of self-control for me not to reply with a big ole sassy eye roll and a, "Ya don't say!"

3. I wouldn't say Josh and I yell at our kids—maybe more like we use loud and firm voices, often and as needed. Since becoming a mom and raising humans, I have found there are loud families and there are soft-spoken families, or as I like to put it, Sriracha families and marmalade families. The Avis family falls firmly in the loud category—we are Sriracha!

Okay, now that you have the background, let's get back to the embarrassing story. Because the summer temperatures in our town often hit triple digits, and because this story takes place during a season when we had two small children who needed to be contained while also being depleted of excess energy, we visited the neighborhood pool as often as our schedules would allow. Pools are great energy sucks for kids.

One afternoon when we showed up at the pool, I noticed that a family we had never seen before was enjoying the cool waters. We gave them a smile, but before we could even say hello, two-year-old Truly bolted from her seat in the wagon I was pulling and headed toward the pool.

"Truly! Stop!" I yelled, as Josh jumped in front of her and scooped her up.

"Oh, so that's Truly?" said the dad of the new family with a sly grin. A statement more than a question.

I looked at him bewildered and a bit creeped out. "How do you know Truly?" Said as more of a statement than a question.

"Oh, I don't," he said, swimming up to the side of the pool where I was slathering Macyn in sunscreen and still giving him a strong side-eye. "We just live a few houses over," he said, "and I hear you yelling her name all the time."

As if on cue, Tru had wiggled her way out of Josh's arms, and we both yelled out, "TRULY!"

When we left the pool that day, I felt completely humiliated and still a tiny bit creeped out that this man had been listening in on what I thought were private moments in our home. But mostly, I felt ashamed that we were always yelling at Truly. Were we always yelling at Truly? Yes, the answer was yes! And it wasn't yelling because we were mad at her or because she was in trouble, although this was sometimes the case. We yelled because Truly entered our lives determined to get all of our attention all of the time. And she quickly discovered she would get more of our attention when she did not listen to us, at least not right away.

When she was in preschool, I was certain she had hearing loss. But when the school did hearing tests for all the students, Truly's came back within the normal range. I actually considered getting a second opinion. She never listened to us! As she's gotten older, things have not changed. I don't know if I'm sorry about this or if I need to embrace it, or both. I do know it all gets extra messy when I compare how I converse with Truly to how my friends converse with their children.

I have this one marmalade friend named Erika, who is so ridiculously sweet and humble and calm and kind that you can't even get annoyed with her for it. You want to, and you may try, but she really is the best. She has six young kids under the age of nine, and she homeschools, and I have never heard her raise her voice with her kids or use a sarcastic tone. I watch her parent, and I'm blown away by how grace filled she is. I am equally blown away at how well her kids hear. Every time they come over and it's time to leave, she says, in almost a whisper, "Okay, guys, it's time to go. Please clean up the toys and put on your shoes." And I'm not joking, every single child stops what they're doing, cleans up the toys, and walks to the door and puts on their shoes. I watch in amazement as Erika continues her conversation with me until all of her kids are lined up and ready to go. It's as miraculous to me as water turned into wine.

When it's just us girlfriends hanging out, Erika tells stories about getting frustrated with her kids and losing her cool. She says she yells at them, but either she's a liar or we have a very different definition of what yelling looks and sounds like.

I cannot tell you the number of times I say to Josh, or my parents, or my friends, or complete strangers, "No one hears me!" as I simultaneously ask the kids to "come here," or "take a seat," or "get in the car," or "stop singing so loudly," or "take a bite," or "stop flipping out." And while I haven't ever finished reading a whole parenting book, I'm pretty sure most of them would say yelling is not the answer. But can we all just take a moment and agree that often it can be pretty darn effective? You do not have to admit this out loud, but I will.

Allow me to share an example, such as the times I need the kids to put on their shoes and head to the door so we can leave. My communication starts out with two simple, clear, and kindly stated instructions: "Put on your shoes please," and "Line up at the door please." And this is not a new concept for them. Putting on their shoes and lining up at the door happens every day, multiple times a day. They need no further instruction. They are capable of these tasks. But do they do it? No.

So how about the second time? Well, I often remind myself that they are small and helpless, and so after a deep breath, I walk toward them, get on their level, look them in the eyes, and say—firmly, but kindly—"Put on your shoes please. Line up at the door please." Then as I step away to grab some last-minute something, I turn around and notice no one is putting on their shoes. No one is lining up at the door. All three are still playing with toys, or dancing or jumping, or just sitting on the floor doing nothing, despite the fact that their shoes are within reach. *Lord, have mercy!*

"DID YOU NOT HEAR ME? PUT ON YOUR SHOES AND GET TO THE DOOR!"

And guess what happens. The kids stop doing whatever it was they were not supposed to be doing, look at me with shock and awe, and move toward the shelf where we keep the shoes. And while a certain, spicy middle daughter ties her shoes, she looks at me and says, "Well, you didn't have to yell at us, Mom."

Really, child? Really?

Sometimes I wonder if their hearing only kicks in once they hear something loudly and for the third time.

There is another listening trick our Sriracha kids play on us—it's known as selective hearing. Let's revisit the example of the simple request to put on shoes and line up at the door. When I know for a fact that the kids can hear me, I sometimes actually lower my voice and completely change what I say. "Hey, kids, who wants a cupcake?" And it is *amazing* how they come running straight toward me with their hands in the air, shouting, *"Me! I want one!"*

"Bummer!" I say back to them. "Now put your tiny shoes on your tiny feet and march those helpless little booties to the door." At least half of the time, the kids give me their own version of an eye roll and head back to their room. But still, catching them in the act of selective hearing offers me a tad bit of satisfaction.

As a mom, I can joke about how my kids choose to listen (or not), but when this same dynamic plays out with adults, it's not so funny. Most of us understand that the way we use our words has the power to hurt or to heal, but I believe the way we choose to listen (or not) also has the power to hurt or to heal.

> **The way we choose to listen (or not) also has the power to hurt or to heal.**

We all allow certain voices of authority to speak into our lives. Whether these authorities are medical professionals, teachers, or political leaders, it's important to recognize that how we understand their advice, wisdom, or rebuke can be tainted by faulty listening. Think about it. How well do we listen when we are afraid, uncertain, or distracted? What happens when we're determined to hear only what we are hoping to hear, or when we plug our ears so we don't have to listen at all? It happens more often than most of us would probably like to admit. When we have faulty listening, we either misinterpret reality or try to curate reality to fit comfortably into our understanding. I've seen this happen in the Down syndrome community, particularly when a person finds out for the first time that a baby has been diagnosed with Down syndrome.

I have interacted with hundreds of mothers of babies with Down syndrome. And regardless of whether they received their child's diagnosis at birth or in utero, their reaction to this unexpected news is almost always the same—total devastation. I have unlimited amounts of grace and love for a mother, or any family member, who feels devastated about their child's diagnosis. It is an unexpected and unplanned shift, and the unexpected is often one of the most terrifying places one can find oneself. But it doesn't have to be this way. We can choose to hear this news differently. In fact, as a shouter of worth for my kids and Down syndrome and for all people with different abilities, I shout in hopes of changing this reaction once and for all.

Decades ago, when there was very little information available about Down syndrome and very few people shouting the worth of these kids, the only voice a new parent heard was that of a doctor delivering a diagnosis. There was no community and no connection to another human being who either shared that diagnosis or cared for someone who did. And for many years, the doctor looked at cells and chromosomes and heart defects and made assumptions about an unknown or dark future instead of looking at that little human being and seeing worth and dignity and hope.

I've spent time with a handful of courageous people who received that news thirty years ago or more when their son or daughter with Down syndrome was born. People who at the time were told the only reasonable option was to put their child in an institution. But instead of listening to the doctor's reasonable option, they listened to their hearts and said, "Over my dead body."

These parents who spoke up thirty years ago are the trailblazers who first began to clear the path I find myself on now, a path leading people with Down syndrome (and the whole world), toward wholeness, acceptance, and generosity. This path still needs to be widened and cleared, and doing so requires those of us who walk it to speak up. I believe one of the main reasons we no longer institutionalize persons with Down syndrome can be attributed to parents who refused to listen to the people who recommended institutionalization and instead insisted that people listen to them as they spoke up against the inhumanity of such an expectation.

So much has changed. Doctors no longer suggest that parents send their children with Down syndrome to an institution. However, the old manner in which a diagnosis is delivered and received remains. It is spoken as bad news, and it is heard as bad news. Perhaps most tragically, when the diagnosis is given prior to birth, many doctors suggest termination.

Let that sink in for a moment.

In the United States, more than half of the women—and in some places as many as 90 percent—who receive a Down syndrome diagnosis in utero, choose to terminate their pregnancy as a result. In other words, there are no other mitigating factors. If the child didn't have Down syndrome, the parents would have chosen to carry the child to full term. That means the Down syndrome community is dealing with a form of modern-day eugenics, which is based largely on misconceptions and unknowns. The most frustrating part of these tragic statistics is that the loudest voices in these future parents' lives are usually medical professionals who know very little about what it means to have a child with Down syndrome.

The moment a woman receives a Down syndrome diagnosis, the very next voice she should hear ought to be that of a parent who has a child with Down syndrome. We parents understand more than anyone the challenges of raising a child with the diagnosis, and we also know what no geneticist could ever grasp about the richness and joy our children have brought, not only to our lives, but to the world. That also means that the only people who should have a say about what it's like living with Down syndrome are people with Down syndrome.

I believe with all my heart that if we listened well and to the right voices, the "devastation" reaction to a Down syndrome diagnosis would no longer be the norm. In fact, I dream of a day when people are not only no longer ignorant about a Down syndrome diagnosis, but also recognize just how lucky they are to receive it. Instead of feeling devastation, I want that mama to high five her doctor! I believe this shift in perspective is possible if we choose to listen to the right voices. But sadly, the voices that need to be heard are either being ignored or sitting silent.

And that, friends, brings us back to Sriracha and marmalade. We need every kind of voice—spicy to sweet—to speak up on behalf of our kids with different abilities. As a Sriracha parent myself, I have no problem speaking up. Most of us who fall in the Sriracha category don't think twice about a little spice on the tongue. However, we Sriracha mamas do need to be careful about using our voices too often or with too much spice.

And for many of the marmalade mamas I know, speaking up is just not on their daily to-do list, or the sweetness on their tongue diminishes the impact of the words they do speak. What I am learning in this whole motherhood journey is that if we want to create a world that makes space for people with Down syndrome—a world that embraces differences and respects and even honors them—then Sriracha and marmalade mamas are going to have to meet somewhere in the middle and work together to become a whole new change-making flavor.

My hero when it comes to whole new flavors that change the world is Martin Luther King Jr. His decision to speak up when it was hard and dangerous not only changed the lives of millions, but it also changed the very world as we know it. In his book *Strength to Love*, Dr. King writes:

> Life at its best is a creative synthesis of opposites in fruitful harmony . . . Jesus recognized the need for blending opposites. He knew that his disciples would face a difficult and hostile world . . . And he gave them a formula for action, "Be ye therefore wise as serpents, and harmless as doves." It is pretty difficult to imagine a single person having, simultaneously, the characteristics of the serpent and the dove, but this is what Jesus expects. We must combine the toughness of the serpent and the softness of the dove, a tough mind and a tender heart.[3]

You can see where I'm going with this, right? It's got Sriracha and marmalade written all over it.

If the Sriracha mama that I am wants to see positive changes take place—in my children, my family, my culture, and the world—then I'm going to need to add a little marmalade to my Sriracha. It may mean approaching school officials who want to put my son or daughter in a special classroom not just with a tough mind but also with a tender heart. It may mean stepping intentionally but gently into conversations with people who do not yet understand the truth that Down syndrome is a gift. It may mean meeting face-to-face with the people who run the Sunday school classes at church to gently yet clearly voice my concerns about the separate classes that segregate people with different abilities and do not honor my children with Down syndrome at all.

And for the marmalade mamas in the room, it's time to reach for the Sriracha! This may mean allowing the compassion you feel for a marginalized person to fuel your engagement in addressing the systems that exclude rather than embrace him or her. It may mean making that poster and showing up to that rally in support of a cause you feel passionately about. From time to time, it may mean finding your voice and shouting as loudly as you can to raise awareness.

We also have to find out how to synthesize our speaking and listening. We cannot only speak, and we cannot only listen. Yes, there is a time to listen and a time to speak, but we still have to do both. When we use the power of our voice and the power of our ears, we can truly begin to make a difference in the world.

Which brings us back to selective hearing. It's not hard for me to see the parallels between my kids and the wider culture when it comes to listening.

I say to my children, "Put on your shoes please and line up at the door."

My children respond, "What? I can't hear you."

I say to my culture, "My child with Down syndrome is not fully accepted in this church, this school, this community."

My culture responds, "What? We can't hear you."

I say to my children, "Who wants a cupcake?"

My children respond, "Me! I want one!"

I say to my culture, "Look at this child with Down syndrome I adopted."

My culture responds, "Wow, you're so amazing! I could never do that."

Why is this? Why does our culture respond sweetly when I tell them my kids with Down syndrome are adopted but ignore me when I raise issues related to their care and inclusion?

Part of it has to do with living in a culture that prizes happiness, comfort, and ease. So we tend to tune our lives to a soundtrack that makes us feel happy, comfortable, and at ease. We may pat ourselves on the back for noticing and talking to that person with Down syndrome or the person in the wheelchair, but that's as far as it goes. We stop short of scooting over to create the space they need to fully belong because it messes with our happy soundtrack.

When we tune our ears only to the voices we want to hear and tune out the voices that make us uncomfortable, we diminish our ability to hear the voice of God. If we make space in our lives for certain kinds of people but not others, we will never know the fullness of God or understand the depths of God's love for humanity.

Just as we mamas want our kids to listen (the first time and with a happy heart, thank you very much!), I think God wants us to listen—to listen to God speaking through the voices of the people we need to hear. And at the same time, I believe God gives us opportunities to speak up and use our voices to create space in our world for the people whose voices aren't heard and who don't yet have a seat at the table.

> *If we make space in our lives for certain kinds of people but not others, we will never know the fullness of God or understand the depths of God's love for humanity.*

It's time to put on our shoes and line up by the door because there is work to be done. When we harmonize both the Sriracha and the marmalade—not only with the words we say, but also with how we say them and the places in which we say them—we create much-needed space for an excluded people group or even an excluded idea. We have an opportunity to create a whole new sweet and spicy seasoning, eager to flavor the spaces in our world where changes need to take place. So let's use our voices in meaningful ways. Let's speak with so much grace and so much force that even our neighbors a few houses down can't help but hear us. Even if they call us out on it the next time we see them at the neighborhood pool.

Chapter 6

DON'T FORGET YOUR PANTS

Dear Macyn,

You may want to kill me when you are a teenager reading this book and see that I shared the following story with the world. Please forgive me. We've both come a long way. You've taught me so much. You are perfect. Never change.

Love, Mom

You may think I'm joking when I tell you that at least once a week, we have to ask one of our children with Down syndrome, "Where are your pants?" Sometimes Macyn will mosey on out of her room half-dressed or totally naked. When I ask, "Where are your pants?" she simply says, "Oh, oh yeah." She then looks down, as though she had no idea they were missing, turns around, and goes back into her room to put them on.

August is still pretty little, and like many small children, he occasionally jets out of the bathroom in a long-sleeve shirt and socks and . . . that's all. I'm in the kitchen chopping cucumbers when I catch a glimpse of his bare buns and yell out, "Hey, buddy, where are your pants?" His usual response is some kind of mischievous laughter as he runs his little bare bottom away from me. Lately, Josh has been no help at all, encouraging August to run through the house in nothing but his birthday suit while yelling, "Streaking!" I remind Josh that it may be funny now, but he'll have to be the one to deal with it when August gets arrested in college for streaking across campus.

Macyn is our most social child. There is nothing she enjoys more than being with people she loves or meeting new people to love. Not too long ago, some friends showed up at our home just as Macyn was planning to get into the bath. We tried to hold her back, but as soon as she heard a knock at the door, she ran to greet them in her birthday suit. When we told her that she had to put clothes on, she melted her naked body to the floor at the thought of missing out on even one second of socializing with our friends. Because the people greeted by a naked Macyn are good friends, we were all able to laugh about it. But there have been times when I wanted to cry instead.

When Macyn was in third grade, we were having a play-date at the park with a new friend who happened to be a boy. I was chatting with his mom when I looked over and saw that Macyn's pants were down. Her friend, who is also in third grade, noticed first. This had never happened before. I didn't know what to say or what to do. He was clearly embarrassed. I ran over to Macyn to figure out what the heck was going on, and she had no reasonable explanation. She just laughed and pulled her pants back up.

The only thing I could think of to say to her friend was, "Sorry!" When I rejoined the mom at the picnic table where we'd been sitting, I couldn't think of one word to say about what had just gone down. The occurrence, while not taught, encouraged, or affirmed, did not take me by surprise. I knew it made the mom uncomfortable—heck, it made me uncomfortable—but I had nothing. So I gave her a simple, "Sorry," and jumped right back in to the conversation we were having before Macyn's pants were down.

The reality is, Macyn and August and many other children with Down syndrome are not always going to meet the expectations placed on them by society. Let's be real here, friends, the *majority* of our kids are not going to be able to meet the expectations placed on them by society. Okay, let's be real real—the majority of *us humans* are not going to be able to meet the expectations placed on us by society. However, a lot of us sure can fake it. Without having to do much bending, flexing, or thinking, we can adjust and fit in as needed. This is not always the case for our kids with Down syndrome or any other intellectual differences, and it's exactly why life can feel so much trickier for those of us raising kids who fail to meet expectations in a more obvious way.

At Macyn's school, the majority of third graders—as in 99.9 percent—would not pull their pants down at the park. (I have done zero studies to get to this percentage, but I'm going to bet it's pretty accurate.) I don't think it's ever a good idea to pull down your pants at the park, and while we've never felt the need to say those exact words to Macyn, at least not until that day, she knows not to do something like that. Let me also add, the majority of third graders with Down syndrome are also not going to pull down their pants at the park. But having been around the Down syndrome block a time or two, and having shared a hundred stories with the mamas and papas I meet around said block, I also know I'm not the only mama who has had to reclothe her child with Down syndrome in a public space.

I've found, as was the case for what I now refer to as the "pants down in the park" incident, that our kids with Down syndrome often are unable to adequately communicate to us why they behave out of the social norm. When I asked Macyn what the heck she was doing and why, she had no explanation.

This was the word-for-word conversation:

Me: "Macyn! What the heck are you doing? Pull up your pants."

Macyn, while pulling up pants: "I don't know."

Me: "Macyn, why did you pull your pants down?"

Macyn: "I don't know."

Me: "You keep your pants on at the park, Macy. You know that!"

Macyn: "Okay."

So, as you can see, she was not very helpful in shedding light on the situation. As a mama raising a kid with Down syndrome, I knew it could be any number of reasons. Her tag was itchy; her undies were bunched up; her pants were too big and started to fall down on their own and she went for it; she wanted a reaction; the wind blew just right, and she had an urge to air things out; she saw a bird in the sky—I don't know, friends. Honestly? So much of raising kids is a guessing game, and when your child responds to the world in a way the world doesn't always understand or make space for, it's a guessing game on steroids.

While the "pants down in the park" incident was a one-time occurrence, every single time I'm in a public space with my kids with Down syndrome, I'm on high alert. At the moment, this is our reality more so for Macyn than for August. August is still little. When it comes to unexpected behavior, there's a lot more grace for toddlers than there is for grade-school children. When a child the size of a two-year-old (which August is, even though he's four) walks up to a stranger and tries to insert himself into a conversation using language that is difficult to understand and maybe even with a little drool on his chin, it's almost adorable. Or when a toddler-size child flops and drops to the floor in the middle of a public space, it may not be adorable, but it's understandable. But when a nine-year-old does it, it is unexpected, and it makes people uncomfortable.

Macyn is famous for asking people, "What's your name?" She's been doing this for years. And while it's a perfectly good and appropriate way to interact with people, she somehow manages to take it to a whole new level.

First, it's more of a passionate demand than it is a question. She never gently or kindly says, "Hi, what's your name?" She just goes right up to any person or group of people, in any situation, and with her tongue slightly thrust forward and her finger in the person's face, she demands with a bit of a low growl, "WHATCHA NAME?"

Second, it's almost always a one-way conversation. For example, she walks up to a group of three people and addresses one of them with, "WHATCHA NAME?"

"Hi," the kind person responds, "my name is Lane. What's your name?"

Macyn then completely ignores the question, rotates her body away from Lane, turns to the next person, and says again, "WHATCHA NAME?"

"My name is Maria. What's your name?"

Once again, Macyn rotates her body away from Maria to the next person, puts a finger in that person's face, and repeats, "WHATCHA NAME?"

"I'm Lucia. What's your name?"

And sometimes, if everyone in the group has given their name, Macyn will say, "Macyn!" Then she moves on. Other times, she never says her name and just moves on.

We've spent a decent amount of time teaching Macyn the best way to have these interactions. Practicing with her as we remind her to stop and tell a person her name when asked and teaching her when it's appropriate or not to approach people and ask their names. These are lessons she is slow to learn or perhaps does not see the need to learn, and so, it makes me uncomfortable every time she walks up to a new group of people. I know how this scenario will unfold, and not everyone is kind about being accosted by a child with Down syndrome—or by any child, for that matter.

Macyn is set on finding out people's names in every situation, but not every situation is appropriate for meeting people. For example, passing people on a busy sidewalk, people getting in their cars in a parking lot, people sitting at a sidewalk café eating lunch with friends, or people sitting in every booth between our table and the door of the restaurant. Most of us know these are not the scenarios in which a person should insert herself, even if it's to ask a person for his or her name. Most of us know these are the kind of scenarios in which it's best for a person to simply smile, nod, or, at most, wave.

Yet, with Macyn, all of the above happen often. We've tried to teach her best practices for how to respond to a person we are passing or to a person getting out of their car in a parking lot. When we role-play and practice with her, she does great. But when an actual human being is in front of her, the temptation for interaction is too strong for her to resist. The majority of the time when she begins her "WHATCHA NAME?" song and dance in an inappropriate social setting, I will say, "Come on, Macyn, we are not asking that right now. Remember, we can wave, smile, and say hi."

Sometimes I can drag her toward our destination with no one being the wiser, but most of the time, as soon as she feels my hand pull her toward me, she digs her heels into the ground or does the notorious Down syndrome flop and drop (mamas and papas raising a kid with Down syndrome, you know what I mean!), bringing a whole new level of social inappropriateness to an already awkward situation.

One time, I was solo with all three kids in a very hip and very cool section of Los Angeles. People in urban settings are usually less patient with my kids and their shenanigans.

And people in Los Angeles, most of the time completely unconsciously, strive for a level of hip and cool that often allows no space for Down syndrome—or even kids, for that matter.

So there I was in downtown LA with all three kids, trying to make it from our car to our destination, which is a bit of a circus sideshow almost every time. Kind of like herding wild cats from point A to point B. I was managing to keep them out of the street and off the ground and out of ice-cream stores when we passed by a very hip, borderline swanky indoor/outdoor café. It was lunchtime, and the place was packed—every single sidewalk table was full.

Macyn started out by simply waving at the people eating lunch and saying, "Hi!" I felt so proud as I watched her put into practice the lessons on social appropriateness we had been working on with her at home. Still, I was on high alert, and so I went to grab her hand, suspecting that her socially acceptable waving might soon turn into a less than socially acceptable, "WHATCHA NAME?"

And sure enough, just as we began to pass the last table and were nearly in the clear, Macyn yanked her hand from mine and approached a table where four very hip people were eating a very hip lunch and began her "WHATCHA NAME?" song and dance.

My shoulders tensed up, and I felt a slow fire begin to build up in my gut and take over my whole body. There are many layers here. One being Macyn's age. Remember, if a toddler approaching a group of people eating lunch at a restaurant begins to strike up a conversation, it straddles the line between adorable and obnoxious, almost always falling on the side of adorable. When a nine-year-old child does the same, it's a lot less adorable. As we know, socially, toddlers get away with much more than nine-year-olds. This is simply the way of the world.

Another layer? Macyn wears her difference on her face. Meaning, as soon as she approaches a group of people, her facial features make it obvious that she is different—and different makes people uncomfortable. Therefore, unless she's approaching a table of people who have a loved one with Down syndrome, which is statistically unlikely—and by the group's reaction we know instantly—before she opens her mouth, the people she is approaching are already feeling some kind of discomfort based solely on the fact that she has Down syndrome and is walking their way. And yes, these thoughts are all going through my mind in the three seconds it takes for her to break away from me and approach the unsuspecting, hip lunch-goers.

Once she begins to interact with the strangers, a whole nother level of unexpected awkwardness opens up. Because she'd already stepped over the line of social appropriateness by approaching a group of strangers eating lunch, the seed of discomfort had been planted. I knew I could predict Macyn's behavior in this scenario, but I could not predict how the people eating lunch would respond. At this point, before she even opened her mouth, I was ready to jump in, believing if I could end the interaction before it took place, I would, in fact, be rescuing Macyn from unnecessary embarrassment and saving these poor, hip, lunch-eating strangers from unnecessary discomfort.

Jean Vanier, the founder of L'Arche, a network of communities that care for and do life with people with different abilities, has seen it all in terms of people's reactions to the perceived social inappropriateness of those such as my sweet girl, Macyn. In his book *Becoming Human*, he comments on why we might avoid or be fearful of interacting with a person who has a different ability: "People with intellectual disabilities . . . seem so different, as if they were in another world; it seems impossible to communicate easily with them. We can feel totally helpless in front of them. Fear of failure, of not coping with a situation, of not being able to relate to another person, is at the heart of this fear of the different, the strange, the stranger. It is as if we are walking in unknown territory."[4]

I think this is true for the majority of people whom Macyn approaches with her "WHATCHA NAME?" routine. In fact, I think this is true for all of us, even those of us who have a loved one with an intellectual disability. We fear the unknown. And unfortunately, until we create space for people with physical or intellectual disabilities to show up exactly as they are and give them permission to interrupt our social norms, they will continue to be unknown and we will continue to be fearful.

Later that afternoon, I sat down with a friend who is a therapist and processed my experience with the hip lunch-goers. When she asked me why I felt the need to control these interactions Macyn has with people, I didn't have a quick answer. But as I continued to process the experience with her, I realized it was my own fear of failure and not knowing how to cope with a situation that would ultimately lead to *my own* discomfort. I felt similar to the unsuspecting people Macyn approached, not because of Macyn and her behavior, but because of the behavior of the strangers. I worried about how they were feeling, how they would respond. Every time Macyn did something that might be perceived as socially inappropriate, I felt as if I was the one walking into unknown territory.

My sweet friend listened to me and then said, "Macyn acting in a way that may not be the social norm does not make it inappropriate. It is not your job to worry about or hold the opinions and reactions of others. Let that stuff go."

This conversation was the first time I had been face-to-face with why I felt so much discomfort in public spaces. It had very little to do with my kids and their behavior, and so much to do with me. I had given too much power to the discomfort and fears of others, and it was time to break those chains.

I thought about the scene at the hip restaurant in Los Angeles, and I replayed the events that made me feel so uncomfortable. While Macyn's interaction with the people eating lunch would not be considered socially "normal," neither was it inappropriate. It was just different. I thought about my girl and how she had radically redefined "normal" for me, and what an honor it is to watch her do the same for everyone who gets to know her. If there is anything Macyn and Down syndrome have taught me, it's that we have to shift our energy from trying to get Macyn and people like her to change and put that energy instead into trying to show the world all the ways *it* should change—starting with being open to a little game of "WHATCHA NAME!?" during your meal.

About a year after I realized why I was so uncomfortable with Macyn and her perceived social inappropriateness, my family and I were having dinner with a friend at a popular restaurant in New York City, right in the heart of Times Square. As it is with every restaurant in Times Square, the place was packed. When we got up to leave at the end of our meal, Macy approached the table nearest to us and interrupted their dinner with a classic round of "WHATCHA NAME!"

The friend we were having dinner with glanced at me with a look of panic in his eyes. Because he was also the person nearest to Macyn, he put his hands on her shoulders and said, "Come on, Macy," and then he gently tried to direct her away, which she resisted. Then he looked at me as if to say, *Do something here!* I smiled, approached Macyn, and smiled at the people eating dinner while I waited for Macyn to finish up getting the names of every person at the table. When she was done, she turned and skipped toward the door and the people continued with their meal.

In the past, I would have felt inclined to apologize for this interaction. I would have been worried about whether Macyn had made them feel uncomfortable and if she had been perceived as behaving rudely. Now I welcome it, knowing that not only is their reaction not mine to hold, but also that these interactions with Macyn—no matter how uncomfortable they may make someone feel—are the very thing needed to begin to make space within our social norms for some necessary abnormal.

Whenever I do begin to tense up because of how Macyn is interacting with the world, I remember the world is better because of her being exactly who she is. The world is better because of the people in it who fully live as the persons God created them to be, feeling little, if any, pressure to change because of the opinions of others. This idea of fully owning who you are in Jesus is something I have seen Macyn, and others with intellectual disabilities, embrace with a boldness and confidence I have been looking to develop in myself my whole life.

I wonder what kind of world we would enjoy if we spent more time interrupting each other's swanky lunches with a, "WHATCHA NAME?" Or stopped to interact with people in the parking lot or took time to interact with those passing us on the sidewalk. What would life look like if we made space for the Macyns in this world to be exactly who they are, allowed them to disrupt the narrow way in which most of us interact with each other? What might the world be like if we spent less time focused on what other people think of us, and/or our kids, and more time focused on learning each other's names?

> The world is better because of the people in it who fully live as the persons God created them to be.

And all of this doesn't pertain only to Macyn. All of my kids have moments when their behavior in public makes my shoulders tense up and I feel embarrassed—moments when I want to deny my kids are mine. Come on, mama, you know what I mean, right? When you're at the park and your kid swipes another kid's toy or pushes a kid down, or falls to the floor, flailing in a fit of rage because they want another Zbar, and you are so tempted to step back and join the other mamas looking on in disgust while simultaneously scanning the crowd for the mother of this hooligan, as the crowd begins to wonder out loud, "Whose kid is this?" If you have never had this experience as a mom, your time will come.

So where do we draw the line when it comes to our child's behavior? I think we can all agree it is inappropriate to throw oneself on the ground when we don't get what we want. Or to hit a person or swipe her things. Or to take our pants off at the park. But what about when a person comes up to us suddenly and wants to interact in a way that invades our personal space? What about when a group is playing together or enjoying a meal and a person approaches and interrupts with their version of "WHATCHA NAME"? What if we chose to engage the people in the world who respond to it differently than we are used to, rather than allow our fears to deter us from interacting? What if we began to see the difference between actions that are inappropriate and actions that simply make us uncomfortable? And what if we chose to embrace the discomfort, to lean into it and learn from it, rather than avoid it?

Down syndrome or not, we risk breaking social norms simply by taking our children into public spaces. Sometimes it seems as if our kids were born for the sole purpose of embarrassing us. While I say this lightheartedly, I also say it with great conviction—our kids are creating opportunities for us to see the world differently all the time.

In my experience, seeing the world differently is not where the challenge or the change is found. The challenge is not how we see the world but rather how we respond to it. As much as it is my hope to avoid another "pants down in the park" incident with any of my kids, it is also my hope that when such incidents occur, we will see how it's not just Macyn who needs to respond differently, but that all of us have a responsibility to shift the way we react when faced with uncomfortable social situations. All of us need to scoot over and make some room for people to respond in a way we're not used to. As we strive to make this world better for ourselves and for our children, I pray we recognize that it is the very people who respond differently than what we're used to who have the most to teach us.

> The challenge is not how we see the world but rather how we respond to it.

Let's continue to encourage our kids to keep their clothes on in public spaces, but let's also remember that this world will benefit greatly if we become the kind of people who take the time to interrupt our days with a good ole "WHATCHA NAME!" from time to time.

Chapter 7

ASSUME COMPETENCE

I 'm sorry."

These two simple words have a vitally important place in our lives. They have great power to heal broken hearts and mend broken relationships. But would you be surprised if I told you these two small yet powerful words that heal and mend also have the power to destroy dreams, break hearts, and sever relationships?

"I'm sorry" are two words no expectant mom or dad wants to hear. When spoken by a doctor—or anyone else—these words create a tangled web of damage for many parents of children with Down syndrome or other different abilities diagnosed in utero or at birth. They choke a parent's hopes and dreams.

I've never been pregnant, but my two sisters have given birth to a total of five babies, and I have attended three of the five births. I happen to adore birth and consider myself a bit of a birth junkie. I think we can all agree that growing a human in another human's body is a mind-blowing experience. And then, when it's that human's time to be born, the body of the woman growing a human begins to open up, all on its own, so said tiny human can be squeezed through her lady parts. It's so freaking wild! A true miracle.

All three of the births I attended were natural births. While my sisters each chose to have their babies in a hospital, they also chose to do it drug-free. I will never forget their bravery and strength as they spent hours in agony, enduring the pain of allowing their bodies to stretch and expand so their children could enter this world. I vividly remember the tears I cried as I watched my sisters breathe and moan and yell through their pain. And I'll never forget the feelings of total euphoria when their hard work produced the fruit of their labor (literally) and my sweet niece or nephew entered this world.

I don't believe there's a word in the English language to adequately express the good feelings one feels when witnessing a birth. Even though I will never experience those feelings as the human who grew the baby, when I couple my birthing-room experiences with the overwhelming adoration and love I feel for my own kids, I can begin to imagine how my sisters felt when their babies were born.

I believe the sweetest moments of a child's birth should be those first hours of life. With my sisters, two of the three births I attended were seamless, and the first hours of those babies' lives were sugary sweet as we sat for hours staring at the tiny little human and then passing him or her around for all the aunties, uncles, and grandparents to breathe in and adore.

Yet not all births are seamless. My oldest nephew was born with pneumonia and quickly rushed to the NICU. Instead of euphoria, there was a heavy feeling of desperation among those of us in the room when he was rolled away. I know that, all too often, babies are rushed to NICUs or to surgery within their first hours. And that is a tragic, albeit necessary, way for their lives to begin.

But do you want to know what is *not* necessary—what should not be allowed—within those first hours of a new baby's life? I'll tell you. It is not necessary to hear the words, "I'm sorry," spoken over a new child. Especially when followed up by, "Your child has Down syndrome," or any other condition. We need to make a permanent separation between these two phrases. In fact, I would like to take this moment to propose we forever ban from our vocabularies the combo of "I'm sorry" and "Your child has Down syndrome." All in favor, raise your right hand and repeat after me, "I will never use the words, 'I'm sorry' and 'your child has Down syndrome' in the same sentence." Good, now we may proceed. When a parent gets an in-utero diagnosis or an at-birth Down syndrome diagnosis, no one in the room should be saying, "I'm sorry," at least not in regard to the extra chromosome their new baby has.

I used to teach special education, and I took a handful of graduate-level classes on the subject of behavior and behavior modification. I've learned we cannot simply remove a behavior; it must be replaced with a new behavior. So, here is a list of appropriate statements we can use in place of, "I'm sorry, but your child has Down syndrome."

- "I'm sorry your vagina hurts."
- "I'm sorry you're going to be tired for the next few months." And then, if you're the sassy type, you may mumble under your breath, "And for the rest of your life."
- "I'm sorry you're going to spend the time between now and the next time you poop, stressed about pooping."
- "I'm sorry your social life is most likely going to be placed on hold."
- "I'm sorry you have hemorrhoids."
- "I'm sorry you're going to be changing diapers for the next three years—if you're lucky."
- "Did I mention how sorry I am that your vagina hurts?"

Unfortunately, these are rarely the "I'm sorry" statements new parents of a child with Down syndrome hear.

Here are some of the *actual* statements made to people I know whose child received a Down syndrome diagnosis:

- "I'm sorry to tell you the prenatal test came back positive for Down syndrome. Let's go upstairs and take care of that."
- "You knew ahead of time the baby had Down syndrome and you kept him?"
- "You need to realize your child won't amount to anything, and her life will have no meaning or purpose. So don't expect too much."
- "This is why we do genetic testing, so we can handle these babies before they are born."

- "Oh, my goodness, I can't believe I didn't catch it. That's never happened to me before. You could have terminated. I'm so sorry." (Spoken by a doctor to a new mother at her baby's one-month follow-up appointment.)
- "You can place your daughter in an institution, you know —a developmental center or group home like our city council member did with her daughter with Down syndrome."

This last statement was spoken to a dear friend by her doctor when her baby was two weeks old. Her daughter is now twenty-eight. My friend made certain that her daughter would not only be raised in a loving home but would also be fully included in a general education classroom for the length of her school career. She blazed a trail for other mamas, such as myself, and showed us what our kids with Down syndrome *can* do.

Friends, a new baby is a gift. Period. A new life with endless possibilities. There is no way to know how any of our children are going to end up, Down syndrome or not. There's a list of reasons not to start a conversation about a child's Down syndrome diagnosis with "I'm sorry," but in my opinion, at the top of that list is this: Saying I'm sorry assumes this child will amount to nothing. It lays a hopeless and tragic foundation for a brand-new baby.

How can any person know the future of a child who is only minutes old? How can we look at a brand-new life and decide if it is valuable or not? How can we look at any child and lay claim to his or her future, predicting it will be hopeless and tragic?

As an adoptive parent, my experience is somewhat different than that of most parents who receive a Down syndrome diagnosis. While Josh and I never set out to adopt a child with Down syndrome, our shock at the idea of being parents of a child with Down syndrome was short-lived. My devastation came with the loss of my fertility. By the time we found out about Macyn, I had mourned that loss and moved on. More importantly, I had learned that there was hope and wholeness on the other side of my loss. Once I let go of my original plans and expectations for my future and fully grasped that motherhood would find me a different way, I was able to adjust with greater ease when other areas of my life took an unexpected turn.

Letting go of expectations and plans is always a shock to the system, but it's important to make a distinction between lost plans and a Down syndrome diagnosis. I believe a parent's initial shock and devastation about a Down syndrome diagnosis is often more about the sudden shift in their plans for the future than it is the diagnosis itself.

It's important to make this distinction so we can more clearly see what exactly it is we are shocked and devastated about. However, it's hard to make any distinctions when the medical professional delivering the news begins with "I'm sorry." Nothing positive follows such an "I'm sorry." It's a phrase followed only by something negative, making it safe to assume that, in addition to mourning the loss of plans and expectations, we also have to brace ourselves for something bad. When a Down syndrome diagnosis is what follows "I'm sorry," it communicates that Down syndrome is bad. As time goes by, parents begin to realize it's not true, but parents have the right to know the truth about their child from day one. And the truth is, Down syndrome is *not* bad.

I believe there are three main reasons it took my husband and me only a few weeks to completely embrace the idea of having a child with Down syndrome.

1. **God's grace.** I believe there is a call on my life, and a key part of that call includes adopting Macyn. It was God's grace that put yes on my tongue and peace and joy about Down syndrome in my heart.

2. **The loss of my fertility.** Through this journey, I had discovered that there was goodness waiting for me on the other side, and that my plans and expectations are not always for the best. By the time I found out about Macyn, I had already been through the tunnel of grief and come out the other side stronger and more willing to step into the unknown.

3. **The fact that "I'm sorry" was never a part of our journey toward Macyn.** Not once did a medical professional, social worker, family member, or friend say, "I'm sorry" about our child with Down syndrome.

When we start with "I'm sorry," it not only sets a negative tone, but it also sets a very low bar for our kids with Down syndrome. And this low bar has the potential to follow our children throughout their lives. When we feel sorry for children within minutes of their birth, it can fog up the lenses through which they are seen, not only by their parents, but also by their schools, churches, and communities.

What if we traded in "I'm sorry" for something like—I don't know, how about, "Congratulations!"? What if we looked at the life of a tiny new baby with Down syndrome and chose to see possibilities rather than losses? What if, from the second our child is born—or from the second a person with Down syndrome enters our life in any capacity—we looked at that person and did something radical? What if we assumed competence? And let's not stop there. What if we did this not only for people with Down syndrome but for everyone?

> What if we looked at the life of a tiny new baby with Down syndrome and chose to see possibilities rather than losses?

Remember Club 21, the nonprofit I mentioned in chapter 4? One of the founders and the current president of Club 21 is a woman named Nancy. Nancy is a woman with kind eyes, a warm presence, and a fierce and spicy personality. I loved her from the very first time I met her. She has been a mentor for me—someone I call on when I get stuck in those deep, dark places only raising children can usher us into. She is my go-to when I need advice or a good talking-to, especially when I doubt myself or my children with Down syndrome. I adore this woman.

When Macyn was in first grade, her schooling began to fall apart. We had transferred her to a new school, a school that was noninclusive, meaning they placed her in a separate class for kids who have different abilities. When we started at this school, I made it known I wanted Macyn to be in a class with her fellow first graders. Because the support she needed in order to be successful in a general education classroom was not available, her educators and I came to a compromise: Macyn would spend social times, such as rug time in the morning or music time in the afternoon in a first-grade general education classroom, and for the rest of her day, she'd be in a special education classroom.

Initially, this setup seemed to be working, but it didn't take long for Macyn to let us know it was decidedly *not* working for her. Because Macyn's verbal communication skills were limited, she communicated through her behaviors. She began to hide under desks and tables, and she'd refuse to come out. She spit on, screamed at, or batted away anyone who tried to get her out. She refused to go to and from places she needed to be on campus.

In the midst of trying to figure out where these behaviors were coming from and what to do about them, I ran into Nancy at a Club 21 event. When she asked how I was doing, I began to cry.

"Oh, Heather," she said as she pulled me aside, sat me down, and put her arm around my shoulder. "What is going on?"

"I don't know what to do with Macyn," I said. "She started spitting and hitting and refusing to leave the classroom or playground." I leaned into Nancy and cried. When Nancy asked about where Macyn spent her time during her school day, I filled her in on our setup.

"Heather, I don't think Macyn knows where she belongs," Nancy said. "I think she's behaving the way she is because she wants citizenship in her classroom, and with all the back and forth between the special ed class and the general ed class, how can she know where she belongs?"

"Oh my gosh, you're right!" I said as I took a deep breath. "I want her in the general ed classroom, but her academic skills are so low I don't know if she can do it."

"Well, that may be true," Nancy said, "but let's start with assuming she can."

This was the moment the foundation of the concept of assuming competence took root in my heart.

There is a serious lack of assumed competence within the education system, and especially for students with an Individualized Educational Plan (IEP). IEPs mean well. They are put into place to make sure students with different abilities have access to a free and appropriate public education. The plan itself is created by a team and is individualized for students who don't fit into the molds of the educational system.

The problem is, IEPs are deficit driven, meaning they start by identifying how far behind students are and what they are unable to do. This effectively places a magnifying glass on all the ways the children aren't making it. While I can understand how this helps identify children's needs within a specific skill set, I'm concerned that focusing first and primarily on their deficit-based needs will keep us from identifying what they really need. And what children with different abilities *really* need is pretty much the same thing every human being needs: acceptance and opportunity—to know their worth and to be seen as able. We do not need to know what a child cannot do in order to meet these core needs.

Josh and I have worked with a lot of teachers who understand these core needs and see only potential in every single one of their students, including our Macyn. And we've worked with a number of educators who first see Down syndrome or a "behavior issue" or a lack of some kind of skill, which inevitably causes them to either miss out on Macy's real needs or blinds them to her abilities and potential.

Children with different abilities need pretty much the same thing every human being needs: acceptance and opportunity.

Here's an example. Macyn has a difficult time with her fine motor skills. She always has, which we know doesn't mean she always will, but not everyone shares our perspective on that. When she was in second grade, she was still just barely able to write her name legibly, and any work that required using a pencil and paper ended up consisting mostly of scribbles. Not being able to write is extremely problematic in school because most assignments only allow a student to demonstrate knowledge of a topic through writing. Which means a student such as Macy is not able to accurately demonstrate what she's learned. So when she was in second grade, we requested something called an assistive technology assessment.

The assessment was simple—a person trained in assistive technology devices observed Macyn in her educational setting and then made recommendations about tools that might help her. Assistive technology for writing can be as simple as a special kind of pencil grip or as complex as a tablet app that "writes" when a student points at words or symbols.

When the assistive technology professional presented her findings, she said, "Because Macyn is not writing, and she probably never will, I recommend she use an iPad with specific writing applications to help her write." Did you catch that? I'm sure she meant well, but in my view, it felt like this educational professional and member of our IEP team had assumed the worst for Macyn.

Before she could say anything else, I interrupted. "Macyn's not writing *yet*," I said, looking her straight in the eye, "but that does not mean she never will."

"Well, yeah, of course," was her quick reply. And the team moved on.

It's a small thing, right? But this is the problem that people with Down syndrome face all the time and in a thousand "small" ways—this idea of "can't." Look, there's a real possibility the assistive technology professional is right—that Macyn *will* always need some kind of assistive device to help her write. But if we tell Macyn this, if we assume this deficit is not only now but forever, especially when she is still so young and has so much potential, are we not in fact setting her up to fail? And why is it somehow acceptable to assume a person with Down syndrome "can't," to essentially assume the worst about him or her, when we wouldn't consider that an acceptable thing to assume about any other group of people? Isn't there precious little to lose and a whole lot to gain by assuming competence instead?

And while we're at it, let's apply this principle to other people in our lives as well, perhaps especially to people groups who are different from us. What were your thoughts the last time you walked up to a group of people whose skin color, culture, or religion is different from yours? What assumptions did you make? Were you able to see them—individually and as a whole—and assume competence? Or was your thinking deficit based?

These are important questions, ones I constantly ask myself. When I choose to look at others and assume competence, I not only allow them room for growth, but I also affirm their dignity and worth as beloved creations of God, the very thing I'm asking people to do when they meet my children with Down syndrome.

My friend Nancy from Club 21 has created a program to make sure this affirmation of dignity and worth happens for new babies with Down syndrome in her community. She has assembled a team of first responders—women who have a child with Down syndrome—to go to hospitals and meet with parents whose child has been given a Down syndrome diagnosis. More often than not, these first responders are the first people to look at a terrified mom and dad and say, "Congratulations!" Sometimes they don't say much more than that because they know this one little word is loaded with assumed competence. Having been terrified new moms themselves, who heard only "I'm sorry" when their children with Down syndrome were born, they know the power that assuming competence can have.

Assuming competence is more than a mind-set or a value; it's more than simply seeing potential ability in a baby born with Down syndrome. It's a posture of the heart—one that forever changes the way we view ourselves, our kids, our neighbors, and, yes, even those who make us feel uncomfortable.

Chapter 8

DANCE!

We sat on an old dark leather couch in one of the small, square rooms in the office of our adoption agency. We were there to meet with my future daughter's birth parents. My palms were sweaty, and I had the feeling that fire ants were marching through my stomach as they told us a little more about themselves.

"I love to dance," said Vickie, our daughter's birth mother, with a smile. "In fact, I danced and listened to music through-out my whole pregnancy." The expression on her face shifted from a smile to a far-off look.

My eyes welled with tears as I envisioned this woman dancing in her kitchen while she cooked, overflowing with the joy of a baby growing in her womb. And then, later, I imagined her doing a slow kind of dance in her living room when the sorrow she felt from a Down syndrome diagnosis led her to create an adoption plan for her baby girl.

I learned a lot about Vickie that day. But the one thing I remember most was the look of pure delight on her face when she shared her love of music and dance. And that's what I was thinking about eight years later when Macyn conquered her first dance recital—a dance recital that changed my life.

Macyn started dancing before she started walking. I have a video of her at eighteen months old scooting around on her tush, a cannula in her nose pumping oxygen to her sick little lungs. And then, as the sound of music makes its way to her ears, she stops dead in her tracks and starts swaying side to side and back and forth. My girl has always loved to dance.

When she was four, we enrolled her in ballet, but it was too slow for my, shall we say, aggressive dancer. I don't recall exactly when it was that Macyn first heard about hip-hop, but I can tell you this: as soon as she did, she was hooked.

I also don't recall why we didn't get her into a hip-hop class until she was eight years old. As it goes with most extracurricular activities and a child with Down syndrome, the first does not usually make space for the second. During those first eight years as Macyn's parents, we quickly discovered that most people think it's best to have a separate place for people with different abilities. A "special" class, if you will. But I knew we weren't going to put Macyn in a special dance class. Our daughter with Down syndrome does not live in some special world, separate from everything and everyone, so she was not going to dance in a separate place.

The challenge for Macy is she lacks many of the skills her eight-year-old dancing peers possess. Her gross motor skills and working memory make it difficult for her to execute dance moves with precision and to remember routines. And a hip-hop class wouldn't be the kind of freestyle dancing Macyn did at home—or at the store, or all the restaurants, or on the sidewalk when a car blasting music passed by. This might explain just a few of the reasons it wasn't until Macyn was eight that we finally signed her up for a hip-hop class.

Once I chose a dance studio, I sent the owner and director of the studio a quick email:

Hi. I am hoping to start my daughter in your hip-hop class. She is a beginner dancer, eight years old, and she has Down syndrome. I wanted to see if you have any questions or concerns about having a student with Down syndrome in your studio. Please let me know how to best move forward. Thank you.

The studio director, Alison, quickly replied:

Thank you for your email. To be totally honest, I do not have very much experience with students who have Down syndrome. That being said, your daughter is welcome in any of the dance classes we offer, and I look forward to working together. Thank you, Alison.

So we showed up. And Macyn loved it. Every Tuesday, she woke up and asked, "What's today? Hip-hop?"

And I would reply in my best announcer voice, "After school, it's time for hiiiiiiip-hoooooop!" Then Macyn would jump up and down, yelling, "Hip-hop! Hip-hop!"

This went on for months. If Macyn was healthy, she was at hip-hop. And every time we showed up, it was glaringly obvious that Macyn was the only different person in the room. Macyn was a different kind of dancer. She didn't catch on to the moves as quickly, nor was she able to remember more than one 8-count at a time. She did not have the sharpest moves, and she struggled to stay in formation.

And she knew it. And it was hard. And at times she felt extremely discouraged. At times she wanted to give up. But she never did, because she's brave like that. And she's used to living in a world that rarely bends or flexes for her—which then requires her to bend and flex as though it's her job. It's a shame, but she's used to it—we all are.

Every Tuesday morning, Macyn woke up excited out of her mind that it was Tuesday. Every Tuesday night, we went to hip-hop. Week after week, month after month. And before we knew it, the recital was right around the corner.

And that's when things got real.

The routine she needed to learn for the recital was extremely difficult. Way, way, way too hard for her. About four weeks before the recital, I sat through the whole class and observed the girls practicing their routine. It was obvious that Macyn did not have it. Not even close. We had been practicing at home, but a routine like the one she needed to perform at the recital could take our Macyn a year or more to grasp, and we had only a little more than a month.

My observations led me to believe this was another situation in which little, if any, thought had been given to how to make Macyn successful in this routine. Although the dance studio was happy to have Macyn take a class, it still existed in a world that doesn't always know how to create spaces for people with different abilities. A world that continues to be blind to the fact that we are all better off when we fully include and do life with people who have different abilities.

I sat there that night watching my daughter struggle with the routine and began to have struggles of my own. I thought about how we had showed up week after week, how Macyn had bravely attempted something she could not achieve at the same pace and rate as her peers, and how it felt as though not one person in that whole dance studio gave a rip about my girl. My soul began to wither, and I was ready to call it quits.

> We are all better off when we fully include and do life with people who have different abilities.

The practice ended, and Macyn and I hopped in the car to go meet Josh, our other two kids, and my folks at our favorite hole-in-the-wall taco joint. As I sat there, staring at my plate of carne asada drenched in lime and smothered in cilantro, my mom knew something was off.

"You doin' okay, Heath?" she asked, leaning in close.

"I don't know," I said, and I began to cry. "Macyn's not getting it. She can't do the dance." The words came out as a weepy whisper as I tried to make sure Macy, who was sitting at the other end of the table, couldn't hear me. "It all just gets to be too much."

I didn't have to explain what I meant. My parents had been on this journey with us from the very first day we brought our daughter home. My dad leaned over and gave my shoulder a big squeeze, and with his head next to mine, he said, "Heather, don't grow weary in doing the right thing."

And I squeezed him back, and we cried.

Once dinner ended, I called my friend Nancy from Club 21, who has traveled this Down syndrome road for a lot longer than I have. I admitted I was frustrated and afraid.

"Nancy, what would you do?" I asked.

"Well, she deserves to dance," Nancy said. "She's worked as hard as, if not harder than, the rest of the class. But I understand you don't want her to look sorely out of place." Nancy paused and then continued. "Heather, you have to contact the head of the dance studio and have a hard conversation. See if together you can come up with a plan."

That night, my weary soul wrote an uncomfortable email to the head of the dance studio, and I did my loving best to share my heart and my concerns. She quickly replied and invited me to meet with her and make a plan. The last line of her email gave me hope: "I don't care about raising up good dancers; I want to raise up good humans!"

And I knew she was my people. I went into the meeting the next day feeling all kinds of nerves, because confrontation is never something I'm excited about, but also feeling all kinds of hope because, based on her closing line, I knew we shared the same end goal.

We met. We created a plan. We both apologized for making assumptions and for not talking sooner in order to ensure Macyn's success from day one. We both owned what we needed to own and agreed that if we were going to make this world go around in the way we wanted our kids to experience it, then we had to tackle this issue together.

Fast-forward a few weeks to the Wednesday before the

recital—the official dress rehearsal. Macyn was so excited to be there. A couple of days earlier, she'd had a chance to go up on the stage and practice her routine. She had been nervous at first, but once she understood what was going on, she relaxed into it and danced her heart out. On this night, there was a new kind of excitement in the air, and everything felt a little more electric. It was almost Macyn's turn to dance. She stood in the on-deck hallway with all of her hip-hop friends. She was excited and smiley and seemed ready. Then it was time to go backstage and line up. Things were a bit confusing and different than they'd been two nights prior. There was some pulling and pushing to get Macyn in her spot on the side of the stage to walk out, and it caught her off guard. Something wasn't right.

She refused to go onstage.

Oh, shoot!

On top of working so hard to get to this moment, we also happened to have twenty people who had paid $20 each to watch Macyn dance for less than three minutes. Twenty people who had been with us on this hip-hop journey for the past year. Twenty people who had cheered us on, held us up, and who continually go hoarse shouting the worth of our girl.

The truth is, when you raise a child who doesn't fit into the majority of spaces in life, you don't just show up for things like hip-hop or gymnastics or church or school. Every time you step outside your front door, time after time, you're going into battle, suiting up in the armor of bravery, grace, and grit in order to say, "Dear world, this person is worthy. Please make room for her." And this message, though simple in concept, requires an incredible amount of energy and heart. Nine years in, we know this journey is possible only because of our good, good God and the people, like our friends and family, who are on it with us.

So, there Macyn and I were backstage, while all the girls in Macyn's hip-hop class were already on the stage. The last eight counts of the song played, and Macyn, who had danced so successfully two days prior, was sitting on the side of the stage, refusing to dance. When the song came to an end, the owner of the studio announced that she wanted to run the routine again and "fix some formations."

"Dear world, this person is worthy. Please make room for her."

I knew the formations were fine. She was thinking of Macyn. She stopped the show in the middle of dress rehearsal to rerun the routine just for Macyn.

The music started again. Still, Macyn refused to dance.

Alison looked at me from across the stage. I shrugged my shoulders because, really, I was at a total loss. Then I walked across the stage to her and said, "Alison, thank you so much for being so flexible to make this work for Macyn. I honestly don't know what to do."

"It's no big deal," Alison said. "I just really want her to dance." She spoke softly as a new group of dancers made their way onto the stage.

"Thank you, Alison," I said, squeezing her shoulder. And then Macyn and I stepped outside.

At this moment, I knew two things for sure.

One, if Macyn decided not to perform in the recital,

I wouldn't be upset about the $400 spent on tickets and $75 on costumes. She would know her value, and our love for her would not change a bit if she decided not to dance.

And two, Macyn needed to dance in this recital. I could see in her eyes and her heart the disappointment and confusion she was feeling. She wanted this so badly, but it was all so dang hard. Macyn needed to dance for Macyn.

Once we were outside, I started to walk toward the car, but something stopped me. I knew if we left and Macyn did not dance, there was no way she would have the courage to perform on the day of the recital. So, we walked around for about twenty minutes. Our conversation was like a broken record. Me asking her if she wanted to go dance. Macyn telling me she couldn't do it. Me telling her she could. Over and over again. I had no idea what to do.

Finally, I took her into the big room where some of the moms and dads were watching. Macyn and I sat in seats on the aisle and watched a few of the other dancers.

"Sweetie, that's what it would look like if you were on the stage. It's not scary. You can do this." My words seemed to fall on deaf ears as Macyn continued to feel too unsure of herself. After a few more dancers finished their routines, Macyn turned to me and announced, "Mama, I wanna dance."

"Okay, baby, let's go tell Miss Alison." I knelt down, looked her straight in the eyes, and said, "And Macyn, you've got this."

I grabbed my baby girl's hand, and we made our way backstage. When we got there, the majority of the girls in her hip-hop class were on deck for one of the ballet routines in which they were also dancing. Their costumes consisted of long cream-colored tutus and full-length gloves. Macyn passed by her peers and walked straight up to Alison.

"I'm ready, Miss Alison," she announced with total confidence.

"Okay," Alison said, looking back at Macyn with a smile. She then started giving orders to some of the dancers and the technicians. "Go find as many of the girls in 'Uptown Funk' as you can. Pull up the music and lighting for 'Uptown Funk.'"

"What? We're going to do 'Uptown Funk' again?" the girls began to murmur.

"Listen," Alison said, looking at the girls in their cream-colored tutus, "we are going to run 'Uptown Funk' again. You can do the dance in the costume you're wearing. You do not have to do this routine again if you don't want to, but we are a team, and we're all in this together."

One of the dancers spoke up. "I'm going to dance again with Macyn."

My eyes began to fill with tears as all the other girls chimed in, "Me too!"

Then it happened. Miss Alison got on the mic. "We're going to run 'Uptown Funk' again." She didn't make a big deal out of it; she just made it happen.

And Macyn walked out onto the stage and got in her spot! The music started, and she danced. I ran into the audience so I could watch, and then I sat there and wept.

There it was, a glimpse of heaven on earth. A dozen little girls in cream-colored tutus and my Macyn in her harem pants and a red crop top, dancing to "Uptown Funk." The hundreds of people involved in this recital bending and flexing and scooting over to make space for my Macyn.

When the routine was over, Macyn ran backstage and with pride and utter joy exclaimed, "Mommy, I did it!" I held her and cried. I hugged Alison, and we cried. And then the show went on.

The whole way home, I wept. My brave and capable daughter sitting in the backseat, beaming with pride.

Two nights later, on the night of the recital, she did it again. This time, with all twenty of our family and friends cheering and weeping. I sat backstage that night waiting for her turn to come. And when she walked out on that stage, every single person backstage stopped what he or she was doing and gathered around to watch her dance and to cheer her on. I stood there in a sea of tulle and sequins, more amazed at my daughter than I ever thought I could be.

The journey to this night was about so much more than a hip-hop routine and a dance recital. This journey was about hours and hours of hard work, hard conversations to shout her worth, and hundreds of tears shed while fighting to create a world in which Macyn can fit. On this night, a whole community of people worked together to create a space in which Macyn could be fully herself and still be fully included—a rare occurrence in our day-to-day lives. Everyone did some bending and flexing and scooting over to make room for Macyn, and we all became better because of it.

I love these words from Jean Vanier: "As a child can teach us about unity and about fidelity and about love, so it is [with] people with disabilities. It's the same sort of beauty and purity in some of these people—it is extraordinary. Our world is not just a world of competition, the weakest and the strongest. Everybody can have their place."[5] *Yes, yes, yes, a place for everybody.*

In a world of competition, you would be correct to assume that a dance studio would be a place where the strongest belong and the weakest are left out. It's a competitive sport. If you want to be a competitive dancer, you must dance a certain way. But the dance studio that God blessed us with chose to embrace Macyn and, in so doing, allowed her to demonstrate how everybody can have a place. Everyone within proximity of her was impacted by the beauty and purity with which she approached dance.

Everyone can have a place. I have the honor of witnessing that truth twice a week as Macyn continues to attend not only her hip-hop class but now a musical theatre class as well. It's not all that complicated. We show up for a dance class, and a dance studio makes space for a different type of dancer, and somehow those two things together have the power to change the lives of so many of us who get to watch it all unfold.

And as I watch it all unfold, as I watch Macyn grow as a dancer, from time to time I go back to that first conversation we had with Vickie. I think about the gift of dance she passed on to Macyn without even realizing it. I think about how she made the effort to show up that day at the adoption agency and share her heart with Josh and me. I think about how there was no way any of us in that tiny office space all those years ago could imagine the magnitude of her decision to show up. And how that decision, coupled with a passion for dance passed down to Macyn from her birth mother, would lead to so many people embracing inclusion and belonging. And how by doing so, we are learning to embrace both the strongest and the weakest, knowing that when we do, we get to witness the extraordinary.

Chapter 9

MAKE ROOM
FOR THE
WILDFLOWERS

Macyn has very good taste in music. When she was in preschool, we had daily dance parties featuring a playlist of all her favorite musicians, including Foster the People, Michael Jackson, and The Head and the Heart. One of her favorite songs was by Arcade Fire, and when we'd get in the car, she'd say, "Coco, Coco, Coco," until I put on their *The Suburbs* album and skipped ahead to number four, "Rococo."

Recently, when one of our friends was giving away a pile of CDs, I noticed Tom Petty's *Wildflowers* album among them. It was an album I knew well because Tom Petty was one of my favorite artists during my late high school and early college days. Plus, my dad was a professional studio musician, and his name is listed in the credits because he played saxophone on a couple of songs. So when I saw the CD, I swiped it up and opened the cover to show my kids their grandpa's name. But more than that, I was excited to introduce my kids, especially Macyn, to Tom Petty.

A few days later, I pulled out the CD and inserted it into the minivan's CD player. When the strum of the guitar blasted through the speakers and Mr. Petty sang out, "You belong among the wildflowers," I looked in the rearview mirror and saw a smile spread across Macyn's face as she bobbed her head to this new tune. And I don't know if it was the familiar guitar strum that brought me back to my younger years or the smile on Macyn's face, or the fact that I am a crier, but as I sang the words, I began to cry.

I had spent hours listening to Tom Petty's music, and his *Wildflowers* album specifically, but it was years ago, before motherhood and before Down syndrome. And like so much in our lives, my chromosomally enhanced daughter in the backseat had been peeling back the layers of familiar things to reveal new truths and new beauty. My experiences as a mother, and especially as a mother of children with Down syndrome, infused the familiar lyrics with a new beauty and new truths. As the final verses blared though the minivan's speakers, I looked at my Macyn in the rearview mirror and shouted, "This is for you, Mace!" And I sang this truth over her:

> You belong among the wildflowers,
> You belong somewhere close to me,
> Far away from your trouble and worries.
> You belong somewhere you feel free.

As I listened to this song and sang it for the first time as a mama, the word that stuck out the most was one I had spent the last several years experiencing in a new way—*belong*. With a family as unique as ours, I often find myself wondering where we belong. When I think about Truly being the only person in our family with brown skin and imagine her future as a woman of color raised by parents who are white, I wonder where she will find her sense of belonging—and how I should contribute to that process.

When I drop off Macyn at dance class, even though the studio has been wonderful and has embraced her, I wonder if she will ever feel a sense of belonging when she is noticeably the only person in the room who has Down syndrome and it's sometimes glaringly obvious she does not fully belong to the group. While August is fully included with his typical peers in his preschool class, from time to time, there are still experiences of incompatibility that leave me wondering where he belongs. And then there's our family as a whole. Put all the unique bits and pieces together—adoption, children of different ethnicities, children of different abilities—and there's a whole nother level of wondering where we belong.

Do we belong among the wildflowers? From where I sit, it feels like we live in a garden sort of world that encourages us to plant ourselves, and our kids, in nice neat rows. Then we are to water daily, pull weeds as needed, and offer plenty of sunshine. And if all we're talking about is flowers, this is a lovely and practical way to grow a garden—one that makes it possible for me to buy bundles of flowers from a local florist to enjoy in my home. I get it.

We grow flowers this way because when we want a tidy bouquet and neatly cut stems, this system works. But what about growing kids? Getting back to the metaphor, when the nice-and-neat system works for us, we usually don't think twice about planting our kids in such a well-ordered garden, and we are happy when they spring up neatly in rows. There is absolutely nothing wrong with this. Life is simply easier when we can effortlessly take root within existing systems. And while easier is not always good, neither is it always bad. We need a little easy in our lives to make it through the day. Every mama wants to see her children grow up to be healthy, to be strong, and to belong. And so we do all we can to plant them in places where we believe this will most likely take place.

My issue with the nice neat garden is that its tidy rows leave no room for the wildflowers—for my wildflowers. But here's the thing. There are people who fit nicely in the well-ordered garden system who are genuinely kind and want to be accommodating, so they start pointing out spaces here and there where we can try to fit in and grow our little patch of wildflowers. Spaces in the corners of the garden, perhaps? So as not to disturb the tidy rows?

The thing with wildflowers is, well, they tend to be a bit wild. Whether planted in a wide-open field or next to the nice neat rows, they are going to grow how they are going to grow. When this happens, the garden flowers that are sprouting up just fine in their nice neat rows begin to place unreasonable expectations on the wildflowers. The invitation for the wildflowers to join the garden, which was initially extended with openness and flexibility, now gives way to pruning and plucking the wildflowers to make them grow more like the garden flowers, or maybe to kicking them out of the garden all together. This dynamic is most evident within the garden we call the school system.

Not to put too fine a point on it, but the majority of the schools in the United States still support segregation—it's called "special education." Walk onto most school campuses, and you'll find a separate classroom for people who have different abilities. Often, the system claims they are not practicing segregation because the students in the special education classes attend lunch, recess, and school assemblies together. They call this "mainstreaming" or "integration," but the reality looks more like a cluster of students being shuffled into these spaces but never being able to actually leave the cluster.

The thing with wild-flowers is, well, they tend to be a bit wild.

How can students who spend their full day in a special education classroom have any kind of citizenship outside their classroom? When the kids in the general education setting don't learn alongside the students in the special education classroom and see them only at lunch or recess, the only thing the system has managed to do is to create a sense of "other," not a sense of belonging. If students are not full citizens of their school, then they are simply visitors when they step outside the special education classroom. These wildflowers are not really planted in the garden at all. Instead, they're isolated into pots where their wild can be kept under control and where they can be moved around the garden whenever necessary so as not to disrupt the neatly planted rows of garden flowers.

I have been very clear with our school about how important inclusion is for Macyn and why. It took us nearly three years of convincing the powers that be that inclusion is the best practice, not only for Macyn, but also for all the students at the school. For almost three years, Macyn had shown up at a school that was convinced she belonged in a special education classroom. For those three years, I did everything I could to prove to the school that Macyn should belong as a full citizen. And when Macyn was not fully included, every time I stepped onto the campus to drop her off or pick her up, I too felt as if I wasn't included. We were both visitors waiting for full citizenship, both trying to prove that we belonged.

Once when I was volunteering at a school event along with a handful of other parents, one of the moms pointed out that she had never seen me at a PTA meeting, and she encouraged me to join them at the next one. I smiled at her and politely declined. But if the timing had been right, I might have said something like this: "If the PTA would support kids like Macyn and assist in our efforts to make the school more inclusive, I wouldn't have to work so hard to get her fully included and I'd have some time to show up at a PTA meeting or two." It's difficult to invest in a school or the PTA when I'm not sure if my child or I even belong there.

When I share our journey through the educational system with others, people tend to say one of two things:

1. Why don't you want Macyn in a special education class? Isn't the regular class too difficult for her?

2. Why in the world do you have to fight so hard for her to be in the general education class? Doesn't everyone already support that? Shouldn't all kids learn together?

My responses to these questions are more or less the same: inclusion isn't about academic ability or social appropriateness; it's about acceptance, belonging, and seeing the worth of every student. The majority of school-age students fit nicely into the existing systems and therefore fail to see the ways students with different abilities are pushed aside. When we function easily within the existing systems, the idea of changing it all up—of scooting over and making some room for the student who does in fact learn very differently from the rest of the class—seems a little bit radical.

But isn't that just what we need? A little bit of radical? Some radical love that leads to radical generosity, that leads to radical thinking, that leads to garden flowers and wildflowers sharing the same soil, the same water, the same sun, and growing up side by side? Both needing to give up a little for the other? Both scooting over to make room for the other?

Just this past week, I sat in a room with all of the educators who work with Macyn, and we agreed to get radical. After almost three years of trying to convince the school Macyn could and should be spending her day in the general education classroom with the proper supports, the whole team finally agreed to give it a go. I wish you all could have seen and felt the room from my perspective. While landing this decision should have been cause for celebration on my part, the room was so heavy I wasn't sure how to respond. The looks on the educators' faces and the shrugs of their shoulders made me wonder if they really believed this could work for our Macy girl, or if they agreed to doing this whole inclusion thing just to get me off their backs.

I get it. We are asking them to take this whole idea of who should learn where and how and turn it on its head. We're asking the team to take a student who is only reading about eighty sight words and teach her alongside kids who are reading full-blown chapter books. We're asking the educational team to create routines and systems for Macyn to be able to transition from activity to activity and location to location with more success and ease. The truth is, the way the classroom is set up does not work for Macyn, and we are telling them she deserves to be a part of it anyway. We are telling them to make it work.

Then there are the other kids in the class. We are asking a whole group of kiddos to flex muscles they never knew they had. We are asking them to extend grace to Macyn for her unexpected behaviors, while also viewing her and respecting her as a friend and peer. We are asking them to bend and flex to find commonalities with a little girl who seems so very different. We are asking them to rethink the way they view and understand humanity all together. We are asking them to step out of their rows and grow a little wild.

This kind of learning, this kind of living, this kind of scooting over and making room, is radical—and it is worthy.

Last year, when Macyn was in second grade, she spent half of her day in the special education class and half in the general education class. It was the first time her general education teacher, Miss Dana, had a student with Down syndrome.

And while the curriculum and standards being taught were not going to work for Macyn without some major modifications, Miss Dana was a pro at radical love. She was the kind of teacher who spent her whole career telling all different kinds of kids, "You are capable," "You are worthy," "You belong here."

That year on World Down Syndrome Day, March 21, Miss Dana put her radical love into practice in a special way. Although Macyn was absent from school that day, Miss Dana sent me a message later that evening letting me know the class had made a special project in honor of the day and in honor of Macyn. She had the students trace one of their hands on a sheet of paper, write their name in the middle of it, cut it out, and glue it onto a long piece of paper. Under each hand, they drew a stem and a leaf and called the whole piece "Macyn's Meadow." Miss Dana said she chose this name because of all the ways Macyn was helping them grow. She saw the wild in Macyn and the nice neat rows of many of her other students, and she created a meadow for all of them to grow together. By allowing Macyn to grow wild in her classroom, Miss Dana was making room for the other students to grow as well. It was magical.

People often think about inclusion for a student with Down syndrome or another different ability as something that will mostly, if not exclusively, have a positive outcome for that student alone. What they fail to understand is what Miss Dana knows—that all students are better off when they can learn alongside a student with a different ability.

In her book *Becoming Wise*, author Krista Tippett interviews the beloved Jean Vanier. Commenting on educational systems, he says, "We must educate people to become capable and to take their place in society. That has value, obviously. But it's not quite the same thing as to educate people to relate, to listen, to help people become themselves. The equilibrium that people with disabilities bring is precisely this equilibrium of the heart."[6]

When we truly welcome all the wildflowers and allow them to grow wild among the nice neat rows of garden flowers, we create an environment in which all the flowers can truly thrive. An inclusive classroom is one in which our children can learn how to relate to one another, how to listen to one another, how to help one another to truly become themselves. Inclusion is best for most students who have a different ability and is best for all the students who do not. But for inclusion to happen, for all our children to experience the kind of "equilibrium of the heart" Vanier describes, all the parents need to believe in and support inclusion. We cannot expect our kids to see the worth and value of learning alongside a student with Down syndrome if we don't see it ourselves. And we cannot expect implementation of the changes needed for inclusion to be done well if only a handful of us mamas and papas are doing the work to make it happen. It's going to require all of us to do the work to make sure our schools and our educators see the beauty that can exist when the wildflowers grow smack-dab in the middle of the nice neat rows.

It has been about a year since I introduced Macyn to Tom Petty. And now, when we get in the car, I don't even have the key in the ignition before she yells at me, "Mom, Tom Petty!" As soon as *Wildflowers* comes blaring through the speakers, a smile spreads across her face, and, without fail, I get all choked up. As she sways from side to side, I think about how thankful I am for the wild ways in which she grows, and the wild ways so many people, including myself, have learned to grow because of her. When she belts out the lyrics, I smile and cry and celebrate the truth behind the words. And when I look in the rearview mirror at Macyn bobbing her head to the music and her eyes connect with mine, I cry tears of joy, knowing that while we wait for the systems in the world to see the value, worth, and dignity of my Macyn, I am just so thankful she belongs to me.

> Inclusion is best for most students who have a different ability and is best for all the students who do not.

Chapter 10

SHOUT THEIR WORTH

When August came home from the hospital, our Instagram account, @TheLuckyFewOfficial, already had a large and loyal following. Many of the people who followed helped fund his adoption through a variety of online fund-raisers we put together. When we posted his birth announcement photo, hundreds of people, all of whom are basically strangers, congratulated us. These people had followed our journey to August so closely and been so supportive that they had started to feel like family, almost like a whole community of aunties and uncles. I love our Instagram followers for this.

The digital family we've built with our life in Instagram squares is extremely special to me. From the moment August came home, I shared him with the world. Day after day, post after post, we all fell head over heels in love with our blue-eyed boy. A few weeks after August came home, I got a message from another mother of a child with Down syndrome. "I have to be honest," she wrote, "I envy what you have with August. I wish I would've had that with our Maya when she was a newborn. I spent the first eight months of her life feeling sad and scared about her Down syndrome diagnosis. I wish I could go back and enjoy her and celebrate her like you do with August. Maya is three now, and I can see I was wrong. She is a gift to our family and to me. I just wish I would've known this truth about Down syndrome when she was born."

This is an all-too-familiar lament I hear from moms all over the world. As I've already said, too many new parents find out about their child's Down syndrome diagnosis with a sense of devastation and negativity, often being advised to terminate the pregnancy. Our children with Down syndrome are born into a world in which their worth goes unnoticed at best. A world in which the majority of people continue to believe a person with Down syndrome is not worthy of life. This is simply tragic.

I wince at the thought of all the people with Down syndrome who were never given a chance at life. And I also wince at the thought of all these sweet mamas and papas spending those first minutes, hours, days, months, and years of their child's life feeling devastated about their child's Down syndrome diagnosis.

There's one more thing I wince at, but it's not exactly easy to talk about. I wince when many in the Christian community consider the high termination rate of babies with Down syndrome an anti-abortion issue. *Deep breath.* Stay with me here. I do believe terminating a pregnancy based solely on a positive Down syndrome diagnosis is a modern-day form of eugenics and a tragedy. But when those of us who are pro-life put all of our energy and focus on the anti-abortion portion of a pro-life worldview, we are only seeing a sliver of what it really means to be pro-life. We're also missing an opportunity to make the changes necessary to truly save the lives of the unborn.

When talking with people about the tragically high termination rate for babies with Down syndrome, they often say something along the lines of, "I knew a woman who got a positive diagnosis and considered an abortion. Thank God, the baby didn't end up even having Down syndrome. But can you imagine? She almost terminated a perfectly healthy child!"

Did you catch it? How *not pro-life* that way of thinking is? Do you see how harmful it is when we say things such as, "Thank God, the baby didn't have Down syndrome"? Or, "We prayed the diagnosis was wrong, and God heard our prayer and healed our child of Down syndrome! Praise him!" Do you see how *not pro-life* those statements are? How such phrases are drenched in the stink of believing a certain kind of baby is better than another kind of baby? Which then implies a certain kind of person is better than another kind of person?

I need to take a quick pause for a moment of total transparency. *Deep breath.* As an advocate who writes and speaks for a living, I've learned that people tend to avoid reading or listening to things that make them uncomfortable or feel bad about themselves. I have to be honest (because, remember, I'm a Sriracha mama!) and let you know that while it's not my intention to stir up those kinds of feelings, it *is* my intention to shout the worth of people with Down syndrome and other different abilities. But sometimes when I shout their worth at the top of my lungs, it makes my listeners or my readers a tad uncomfortable. So that's the total transparency about me—I'm just doing my worth-shouting thing. Are we good? I hope so! At this point, we've spent some serious time together in this book, and I'm betting we are both the kind of people who are willing to embrace some discomfort as we walk the path toward growth.

Let us proceed!

We've talked about the typical in-utero diagnosis story for a person with Down syndrome, so let's move on and consider the world the child lives in once he or she is born. Take a moment to think about the places you routinely travel within your neighborhood and community. Do you see Down syndrome? If so, where? Most of the time when I pose this question, people draw a blank. Why? Because for the most part, we live in a world that doesn't create the spaces necessary for people with Down syndrome to live and thrive where they are. The systems may make some room for the person with Down syndrome who is considered "high-functioning," a person who more easily fits into the spaces that already exist in our systems. But most of the time, our communities create separate spaces—special programs or classes—for people with Down syndrome.

Just this past week, I had a conversation about this with a woman while sitting in the waiting room of our chiropractor. She told me about her kids, who attend the high school in the same district we live in, and then asked, "Do you have any kids in the district?"

"Yes, I do," I said with a smile. "I have a daughter at Mayflower, one at Monroe, and a son at Canyon."

"Whoa!" she gasped, "I remember those days. You're all over the place! We were at Mayflower. Good school. You like it?"

This always feels like a trick question. When families move and have the privilege of choosing where they will live, often the item at the top of the list of determining factors is how good the schools are. We've moved a few times with our kids, and when we tell people where we'll be living, they'll often say, "Oh yeah! They've got great schools." The thing about "great schools" that isn't always so great is the measuring stick used to determine said greatness. Usually the measure of greatness is based on one or two things, such as academics and sports or college admission rates. Have you ever heard of a school that was considered great, even in part, by the measure of its inclusion policies? Me neither. If we want to identify a truly great school, we need to use multiple kinds of measurement, because it's only great if it's great for multiple kinds of people.

Back to my conversation with the woman in the waiting room at the chiropractor.

"Mayflower has been a challenge for us," I said. "My daughter has Down syndrome, and we want her fully included in her school, but this is a noninclusive district."

"Really?" the woman said raising her eyebrows in surprise. "I didn't know that. Maybe things have changed, because when my boys were there, I remember there were students like that on campus."

"Oh, yes," I said. "Students with different abilities are on campus, but they're in separate classes, not fully included." I knew the chiropractor would be calling my name any minute, so I spoke quickly. "We believe our daughter has the right to learn alongside her peers, not in a separate classroom for people with different abilities."

The woman gave me an inquisitive look. "Oh, I see!" She should have left it there, but she went on. "But sometimes kids like that need to be together, you know, to be around people who are like them. It's better for them." She said it matter-of-factly, as if she knew it to be true.

While the Sriracha mama in me wanted to spew hot sauce all over her false and harmful ideology, I remembered the importance of blending my Sriracha ways with marmalade restraint and gently yet firmly informed her, "Actually, studies show that learning alongside her peers is the best way for my daughter with Down syndrome and everyone else to learn. An inclusive education is the best kind of education for all kinds of kids."

"Heather?" the chiropractor called my name. I'm pretty sure the woman was relieved the conversation was over. Sriracha mama that I am, I could have gone a few more rounds.

My experience has been that most people think as this woman did—that it is good and necessary for my son and daughter with Down syndrome, and others like them, to have separate programs and spaces in which they can learn and grow. What they don't seem to realize is how this way of thinking communicates to the people with Down syndrome that they are not worthy of participating in the same life with everyone else.

Once again, can you see it—how *not pro-life* this way of thinking and living is? If we're going to stand for life, then do we get to decide what kind of life we stand for? *No!* No, we don't. If we stand for life, then we stand for life. And if we say we are pro-life, then we better be pro–Down syndrome— and pro–black lives, pro-autism, pro-immigrant, and pro-person-with-a-physical-different-ability who still cannot enter a building (maybe even their community church) because it does not accommodate their specific mode of mobility. And if we say we are pro–Down syndrome, then we better be making darn well sure that people with Down syndrome have a place in this world to be fully embraced just as they are.

Every day we have opportunities to step into our schools, dance studios, workplaces, Girl Scout troops, and even churches and make sure all kinds of people fit in those places. We have opportunities to scoot over and make some space, not only for people with Down syndrome, but also for racial minority groups, immigrants, and people with different abilities, just to name a few.

Still with me here? Do you see how pro-life is about so much more than being anti-abortion? It's about shouting the worth of all lives! And especially the lives of those whose worth continues to be questioned. So let's briefly jump back to the mama who finds out that her new baby has Down syndrome. What if that mama saw how well the world cared for people with Down syndrome? What if she saw us demanding that the systems in place include people with Down syndrome? What if she saw us welcoming and enjoying people with Down syndrome? Don't you think this mama would look at her baby differently as a result? If all of us made the choice to shout the worth of people with Down syndrome, this new mama would look at her baby differently because she would see that people like her baby were included at every stage in life and in every space, and they were seen as loved, valued, worthy.

I believe the church—the collective whole of those who love Jesus, follow his teachings, and meet together with a unified purpose to show our love for God and each other—has a powerful and important opportunity to share the love of Jesus with the world by shouting the worth of those who the world still sees as unworthy. If the church adopted a *holistic*, pro-life stance, affirming the worth not only of the unborn but also the born—especially those who are still viewed with a negative lens—the world in which we live would be radically changed.

> Do you see how pro-life is about so much more than being anti-abortion? It's about shouting the worth of all lives!

The truth is, Down syndrome is a small portion of the community of people with different abilities. According to the American Disability Act (ADA), more than 54 million adults live with some kind of different ability. That's one in five. That's 54 million adults who are image bearers of God, who are fearfully and wonderfully made, who are people we may be missing out on knowing because the systems in which the rest of us so easily fit continue to fail to make room for those who don't. In fact, many of these people are unable to successfully access their neighborhood church, a fact that many of us can't even see.

I wonder, then, if it's even possible to know God fully if we are not in a relationship with all the image bearers of God.

We will need to make space in our systems and our lives for people with different abilities so that we have opportunities to see and understand God's heart in new and powerful ways.

I have learned so much from my kids over the years as I've stepped into spaces I didn't know existed. And the longer I linger in these spaces, the more I've been exposed to the injustices people such as my kids are expected to live with. And the more exposure I have to these injustices, the more determined I am to be an advocate for change, to shout the worth of my children and others who continue to be seen as less worthy based on their ability or the color of their skin.

> We will need to make space for people with different abilities so that we have opportunities to see and understand God's heart in new and powerful ways.

Once, during a podcast interview, I was asked if I had always been an advocate or if I had character traits that naturally led me to advocacy. Before the interviewer asked the question, I hadn't thought about it much. When I look back on my childhood, I can see I always had a heart for the underdog. I believe this is because I often felt like an underdog myself. Maybe it's because I'm a middle child (and all the middle children nodded their heads), or maybe it's because I'm an Enneagram Two (and all the Enneagram Twos nodded their heads). But I really do believe that God was preparing me, even in childhood, to be a shouter of worth with a voice loud enough to step up onto a platform when needed.

It seems to me that advocacy is something very few people actually seek out, as was the case for me. Being an advocate is almost always emotionally, physically, mentally, and spiritually exhausting. It's a heck of a lot easier to live within our bubbles—where everyone looks and thinks and acts like us—than it is to burst those bubbles. But do you know what happens when you live inside a bubble? It blurs your vision on everything outside the bubble. In other words, you can't see straight. And if our view of people who are different from us is blurry, then our view of God is blurry as well.

As a middle-class physically and intellectually abled white woman, I was born into a pretty sweet little bubble. It wasn't until I took some trips outside the United States in my younger years and then later adopted Macyn, Truly, and August that I could recognize I'd been living in a bubble at all. Once I could see the world a little more clearly, once I saw how the systems that had worked just fine for me didn't work for my kids and so many others, I could no longer sit comfortably in silence. And that's how and when I became an advocate. No, we rarely go looking for advocacy; rather she comes popping our bubbles and pounding on our door, and given the reality of our circumstances, we gladly let her in.

It's only when our circumstances do not require advocacy that we get to decide whether we want to be an advocate. And that ability to choose advocacy is a privilege—a privilege I once possessed, before kids with Down syndrome or dark skin entered my life. Before Macyn, Truly, and August, when I saw certain injustices happening in the world, I could choose to raise my voice in opposition, or I could choose to remain quiet. But now that these three babes are in my life, there's no question what my response will be when a person or a system treats my kids as less than fully worthy—I am going to advocate for them by shouting their worth at the top of my lungs.

Jesus was the greatest advocate and shouter of worth to ever live. He entered the systems in place during his time on earth, and he said, "Nuh-uh! This is *not* going to work, friends." (This exact wording may not be found in the Bible.) His radical love of the underdog had all the system makers seething (remember the Pharisees?). He taught some pretty out-there stuff, such as love your enemy; forgive unconditionally; leave the many to save the one; people outside your ethnicity/gender/culture are your equals—these were, and let's be honest, still are, radical ideas. And he spent the majority of his ministry life on earth with the people who did not fit or even have access to the systems in place—women, people with leprosy, those who were differently abled, and so many other outcasts of society.

> Jesus was the greatest advocate and shouter of worth to ever live.

Jesus was radically pro-underdog. He was and is the greatest shouter of worth.

So if we love Jesus, if we are familiar with his work on earth, then we can no longer say we don't know. Because we know. And if we know, then we have the great privilege of choosing to step boldly into our roles as advocates for others. As people who love Jesus and strive to be more like him, none of us get to sit this one out. Advocacy is not only for those of us born into a privileged space; it is for everyone. Even if you are among those who need others to shout your worth, there is someone sitting behind you who needs you to shout theirs.

Just imagine, then, a whole world of people who love radically, who live a lifestyle of looking beyond their bubbles to see who's left out, who scoot over to make some room, who shout at the top of their lungs, *I see your worth! You are worthy of life! Worthy of a place to live! Worthy of an education! Worthy of a job! Worthy of our love! Worthy of our forgiveness! Worthy of our positive assumptions!*

When we use our voices to shout the worth of others, it drowns out all the other voices, and the world hears just one thing—the love of Jesus!

Chapter 11

SIT IN THE TENSION

I was in my husband's office at work, hiding away and trying to get some writing done when a friend passed by the window, saw me through the glass, jumped up and down, and rushed in to say hi. Many of my husband's coworkers are also some of our dearest friends, so it's impossible to be in his office and not see a friend or five.

Honestly, I had very little time to write that afternoon, and I was hoping to avoid contact with anyone so I could get some words on paper.

"Heather!" my friend Christine cried out as she ran through the door and gave me a huge hug. "What are you doing here?"

"Christine!" I hugged her tight. "I miss you!"

Our lives had been busy, and we had not had a moment to catch up for weeks, so I knew I wouldn't be getting any more writing done that hour. We chatted a bit and shared what was new with our kids and new at work. We told each other a dozen times how much we missed each other. And just when I thought our conversation was coming to a close, Christine said, "Oh, Heather, I have something I've been meaning to talk to you about." Her words came out slowly and hesitantly. "But I know you have to go so we can talk another time."

I did need to go, but I was too intrigued to end our conversation. "Well, when you say it like that, you *have* to tell me," I said.

Christine went on to tell me how much she loved my first book, *The Lucky Few,* and how it had changed her life. However, the more she went on about how amazing the book was, the more certain I was that there was a big "but" looming on the horizon. I could tell she was uncomfortable with what she was about to say, and I could feel the tension as a knot of anticipation began to form in my stomach.

"As a woman of color, there were a few instances in which the way you described a person in the book made me feel like an 'other,'" she said gently.

My stomach dropped. "Okay," I said.

"It wasn't super obvious, but there were a few places where you use skin color and other ethnically driven descriptors to describe non-Caucasian people, but you never described people as being Caucasian."

As soon as she said it, I knew exactly the sections of the book she was referring to. The knot in my stomach tightened.

"When you describe only people who are non-Caucasian, it implies that all the other people who aren't given specific ethnic descriptors are white. As a woman of color, this just makes me feel like an 'other.'" She paused and looked at me with great concern. "Do you know what I mean?"

"Yes, I do."

And I did. Even so, there was a part of me that wanted to justify my words, wanted to tell her she was being overly sensitive, wanted to defend my good intentions. But I didn't, because I knew better.

In the previous five years, I had been doing intentional work to get outside my bubble—to be in relationship with people who don't look like me, think like me, act like me, or vote like me. I had learned how to sit and listen. I had learned how one person's experience and view of the world does not negate another's. I had learned how much I still have to learn. And because I had practiced the art of listening and learning, I recognized that the need I felt to defend myself had less to do with my good intentions and more to do with my pride.

> I had learned how one person's experience and view of the world does not negate another's.

The truth was, she was right. When I wrote about the characters in my first book, it never crossed my mind to describe the physical attributes of anyone who was white. That's inside-the-bubble blindness, which in this case showed up as normative whiteness. And it's a reflection of my own white privilege.

White privilege is a systemic privilege. That means I don't have to be aware of it or seek it out to benefit from it. White privilege is a holdover from decades and centuries when white people had access to rights and privileges that people of color did not. This isn't to say that all people who are white are making it in life with ease and comfort. What it means is that even if I am the poorest, most struggling white person, I will still receive the benefit of the doubt when I walk into a store or a bank or am stopped by law enforcement. It means I will not be presumed untrustworthy, deficient, unskilled, or dangerous, no matter what I wear, how hard I work, or what choices I make. It means I can describe the physical traits of people of color in my book, yet never think to do the same for people who are white—and the white people reading the book never notice because our whiteness is assumed. It is the standard by which we live our lives, as well as the unspoken standard by which people of color are expected to live theirs.

It was wrong for me to use ethnically descriptive words for only our Latino nurse and our Egyptian doctor and not for our fair-skinned Caucasian nurse. As a white woman telling my story, I never considered how my failure to describe a character as Caucasian placed all the other characters I did describe in a category called "other." It was a blind spot I wish had been pointed out before the book was published for all the world to read. Christine spoke the truth. And this truth made me feel awful.

All my awful feelings sprang from wounded pride. I knew I was wrong and she was right. I didn't know what was worse—that thousands of people had read the book, noticed what Christine noticed, and yet said nothing, or that thousands had read the book and *not* noticed what Christine noticed.

I am so thankful my friend was loving enough and brave enough to speak truth. I know how difficult it can be to shine the light of truth on someone else's blind spot, to point out the fault of someone you love. And yet when we fail to do so because of the possible hurt or awkwardness it may cause, we only allow the blind spots of the world to perpetuate unhealthy relationships.

I also know she was able to share this with me, and I was able to receive it, because we had been investing in each other's lives. We had been eating meals together, celebrating life together, and showing up for each other when things were especially tough. Because we come from different ethnic and cultural backgrounds, doing life together in this way takes some extra work—extra listening and learning and understanding. Extra guts and extra grace upon grace upon grace. We've both been upfront about our desire to do life with people who have a different ethnicity than we do, and because of our commitment to one another, we were able to have difficult conversations when needed. As the Bible says, "Wounds from a friend can be trusted" (Proverbs 27:6).

I haven't always been able to sit quietly in such tense moments and difficult conversations, nor have I always been brave enough to address issues that can create discomfort and tension. I lost a friendship because I wasn't brave enough to speak the truth required for our friendship to be made whole and strong, and my friend wasn't willing to sit in the tension long enough to work it out. Instead, we avoided any kind of tension and our friendship faded over time, which left me feeling wounded, confused, and regretful. Friends, we have to be willing to sit in the tension. Otherwise, we'll end up spending a lot of energy and time avoiding it entirely, which will only leave us with shallow and vain relationships.

Am I the only one who wonders if we've lost the art of

difficult conversation in large part because it's easier to bellow our beliefs without consequence on social media platforms? Think about it. These platforms were designed to connect us, but they can also make it more difficult to connect in a truly meaningful way. Ever see a post that used a small sliver of information to create a whole narrative—one that was hurtful, threatening, and untrue? How often have you come across or experienced a meaningful online dialogue, one that helped you listen and grow? Do you routinely see comments that invite others to "tell me more," or is every post a competition to see who can shout the loudest, sometimes simply for the sake of being loud? Social media platforms have given us an outlet for the tension that properly belongs in—and is necessary for—the healthy growth of real relationships. When there's no room for tension or conflict in our relationships, we are left stagnant in our misunderstandings, frustrations, and self-righteousness.

I have a friend named John Williams who has mastered the art of sitting in the tension. He is committed to racial reconciliation. In fact, his full-time job is to run a center for racial reconciliation. Race is often a very intense topic, and rightfully so. People of all races tend to hold on to and experience different narratives, many of us refusing to look past our own experiences and views to try to truly understand the perspectives of someone outside of our race. Quite often, people who don't understand John's way of thinking or who disagree with him on an issue will post a comment on a social media outlet or send him an email. John always replies with an invitation to coffee. I love this, because not only is he making the wise choice to avoid engaging in social media "dialogue" or to respond quickly and easily with an email; he is also setting himself up to sit in what is likely to be a very tense conversation.

As part of his work, John leads a racial reconciliation workshop designed to introduce participants to the deceptive and destructive effects of racism in our lives and in the body of Christ and to provide opportunities to practice racial reconciliation within a biblical framework. Because the issues of racism are so divisive and personal, those who attend, who are from all different ethnic backgrounds, experience the workshop in many different ways. An important aspect of the workshop is to look at the advantages of whiteness and the disadvantages of non-whiteness within the systems in place in the United States.

When a workshop is over, participants are given feedback forms, which are collected and reviewed by John and his team. Even though people who attend the workshop are given an opportunity for feedback, it's not uncommon for John's email box to fill up with critical emails from workshop participants who feel defensive about their whiteness. They question the integrity of the workshop, criticize John, and defend their way of thinking. More often than not, the people who send these emails are more intent on proving they are right and John is wrong than they are on continuing the dialogue and seeking to understand. Still, every single time, John replies with an invitation to meet, even though he recognizes that because he is an African American and the other person is white, the unrecognized dynamic of bias means that John will not be equally situated at the table—he will have to work harder to be understood or to be heard at all.

So why does John keep extending invitations and showing up? Because he knows it's only through this hard work of racial reconciliation that growth and healing can take place. He knows we have to be willing to sit in the tension rather than pick up our agendas and bail if we want things to change. The healing we long for in the area of race will never be found in social media or any other digital space. We must be willing to sit across from the people whom we understand the least, and even the people who offend us the most, in order to build the bridges of understanding that can lead to the healing we seek.

> We must be willing to sit across from the people whom we understand the least, and even the people who offend us the most, in order to build the bridges of understanding that can lead to the healing we seek.

Once again, Jesus is our example. Some of my favorite stories in the Bible are the ones that show Jesus creating tense and awkward situations on purpose. He shares a meal with a despised tax collector. He heals people who are considered untouchable by actually touching them. He chooses to esteem human beings more highly than the law by healing people on the Sabbath, and then he challenges those who condemn him for doing so. Can you imagine how the twelve disciples might have responded to all this? It's hard not to laugh when I think about it. I picture the Twelve constantly giving him major side-eye as they step into yet another wild and awkward situation, all of them with thought bubbles over their heads that read, *Welp, here we go again!*

One of my favorite awkward moments is when Jesus converses with a woman at a well (John 4:4–26). In this story, the disciples have gone off to find food and Jesus is resting alone by a well when a woman approaches to draw water. The story plays out like this:

"Will you give me a drink?" Jesus asks.

The woman says, "You are a Jew and I am a Samaritan woman. How can you ask me for a drink?"

This is awkward for a couple of reasons. One, because Jesus should not have been talking to a woman alone, and two, because she has a different ethnicity than Jesus does, and Samaritans were despised by Jews. Those two facts alone made this whole situation taboo. I can practically feel the tension rise in her, the knot that began to form in her stomach when Jesus not only acknowledged her but spoke to her and even asked for her help. Later, he takes things to a whole new level of awkward when he plainly states the shameful truth about her: "You have had five husbands, and the man you now have is not your husband." *Gulp.* Definitely not polite conversation.

I love how Jesus just goes there, never beating around the bush, never avoiding the tension, but just going straight to the heart of things, knowing it's the only way true healing and wholeness can happen.

My absolute favorite part of this story happens toward the end. As Jesus is wrapping up this awkward, tense, life-changing conversation, his disciples return from grocery shopping and are "surprised to find him talking with a woman." But get this, no one says a word! No one asks, "Why are you talking with her?" Ha! This scene always makes me laugh out loud. I like to imagine that at least one of the disciples was about to say something when another one elbowed him, shaking his head as if to say, "Dude, you know better than to question what's going on here. Just go with it."

And this is just one of the many socially inappropriate interactions Jesus had. So much of his ministry here on earth was one awkward situation followed by another tense situation, followed by something totally confusing and socially inappropriate. It makes me think of the times Macyn does her "WHATCHA NAME?" song and dance, and how these interactions with her can create some awkward tension, and how there's always the potential for relationship and wholeness and healing for anyone willing to enter the tension rather than awkwardly laugh it away or avoid it all together. It's a truth I try to remember every time I find myself facing anything awkward.

Speaking of awkward, some of my tensest motherhood moments have happened in connection with our adoptions, two of which were open adoptions. Sitting in a room with the people who gave life to the child you hope to adopt is as tense and awkward as you might imagine. And conversation with our small children on the topic of their own adoptions is right up there on the tension scale.

I'll never forget the first time Truly asked me about her birth mother. We were driving on California's I-210 freeway headed toward Monrovia to visit Josh at work. All three kids were buckled in their car seats. Macyn was six; Truly was three; and August was just a wee babe. My cell phone rang, and I saw Macyn's birth mother's name on the screen. I picked up the call through Bluetooth and our conversation was on speaker for all the car to hear.

Macyn's birth mother had called to invite us to an event at her parents' home. We chatted a bit about how she and her daughter were doing, and I quickly caught her up on how Macyn was doing. I hung up the phone just as we were pulling off the freeway. Sweet little Truly made eye contact with me through the rearview mirror and innocently asked, "Who was that, Mommy?"

"That was Miss Vickie, Macyn's birth mom," I said. "You've met her. Do you remember?"

Truly shook her head. "What's a birth mom?" A fair question for anyone to ask, and especially for a three-year-old to ask.

"Well . . ." I was surprised by my own hesitation. "Remember, we've talked about this before? You and Macyn and Augie did not grow in Mommy's tummy because Daddy and I adopted you. A birth mom is the woman who grew you in her tummy." While this was not the first time we had spoken about our children's birth parents, it was the first time she had asked about it.

She sat quietly in the backseat, which was rare for our Truly Star. When she did speak up, the words were too heavy for a three-year-old to hold. "Where is my birth mom?"

And for the first time in a long time, I found myself scrambling for words. I was not ready. The truth felt way too heavy for any three-year-old, but I knew making up a story would be a disservice to us all. She had a right to know her own story, but parts of that story need to be shared when she is older and mature enough to understand and process them.

I answered the question as truthfully and age appropriately as I could.

"Oh, sweetheart, I don't know where your birth mom is." I pulled the car over to the side of the road and turned to look her in the eyes.

"But why do we see Macyn's birth mom and not mine?"

"Well, honey, because we don't know where she is. If we knew where she was, I would hope we could see her. But we don't know. Do you understand?"

Even this brief conversation felt like too much for my tender little three-year-old. I was ready to move on, but Truly was not. "I wish I could see my birth mom." Her little eyes began to fill with tears.

"Oh, sweetheart!" I reached my hand back to grab hers, my light skin and her brown skin interlaced together. "Me too," I said. "And I know it makes you sad. It makes me sad too. I am so sorry it's this way."

She remained motionless, listening to my words and crying.

"But, Truly, you know what? Even though we don't know what she looks like or where she is, I bet you she has the same big, brown, sparkly eyes as you!"

Truly looked up from her lap and gave me a coy smile.

"And you know what else?"

"What?" her smile grew.

"I bet you she has the same beautiful brown skin as you."

"Do you think she has curly hair?"

"Yup! And I know you've never met her, but the two of you got to spend a whole nine months together while you were growing in her tummy. You were together nonstop for those nine months. And I bet she sang to you and talked to you and you could hear her heartbeat. I bet those were some of the best months of her life."

I could see Truly's big brown eyes gaze out the window as she tried to wrap her mind around a topic much too big for any three-year-old. Heck, adoption and the loss from which every adoption plan starts are too much for any person, no matter their age.

This wasn't the last time our Truly Star would inquire about her birth mother. Truly is an inquisitive kid, and she's also in a unique situation. You see, we have close relationships with both of her siblings' birth parents. And to complicate an already complicated situation, Truly is the only sibling who does not have Down syndrome, and the only person in the family with brown skin and curly hair.

To be totally honest, her father and I are constantly guessing about how to navigate the whole situation. We've never done this before. There are books on adoption, and we ask lots and lots of questions of anyone who is willing to answer. Recently, I met a woman at a baby shower who told me she had been adopted as an infant. I didn't let the fact we had just met deter me from asking what some might consider completely inappropriate questions of a person I'd just met. I went in fast, and I went in deep.

"Tell me your story!"

"Do you mind if I ask you some questions?"

"Did you always know you were adopted?"

"How did your parents talk to you about adoption?"

"Is there something you wish they did differently?"

These poor adult adoptees who find themselves in a conversation with me are always so very kind and generous. I'm thankful for their openness as I try to do my very best to learn from them.

No matter how many books I read on the topic and how many adoptive parents or adoptees I talk to, navigating this part of our story always feels like walking across a frozen lake on a warm day. We're just praying we don't fall through and drown in the icy waters below.

Some days we feel as though we're just barely making it as parents. Every day we rely on God's grace to get us through.

When prospective parents are in the beginning stages of adoption, a lot of them reach out to ask us questions about birth family relationships. I've found that the majority of parents have the same desires I had during our first adoption. Most people creating an adoption plan are pretty freaked out about having a relationship with their future child's birth family. My advice is always to hold things loosely because if there's one truth about an adoption plan, it's this—no two are the same. If a relationship with the birth parents is possible and safe, it will be good for everyone involved and should be pursued, even if the adoptive parent feels negatively about the idea.

In parenting, and especially with adoption, we will inevitably need to adjust our plans. For the first five years of Truly's life, we were completely open about our relationship with our other two kids' birth families. When we were invited to spend New Year's Day with Macyn's birth family, the whole Avis clan showed up. When August entered the picture, a few months after he was born, his birth mother asked if she could visit and bring her family to meet him. Her whole crew was welcomed into our home by my whole crew. And when Truly or Macyn inquired about who was who and why they were there, we answered truthfully. This story is their truth, and we're not ashamed of the people involved.

When August was three, his birth mother's parents were in town and stopped by our home for a visit. Within the first few minutes, Truly, who was sitting on the couch next to August's birth mother, blurted out, "Why can't we see my birth mom?"

It is a perfectly fair question. A question we had discussed on many occasions. A question we were happy to talk about as much as Truly needed us to, but not right then, not in front of one of our other children's birth mothers and her parents.

"Good question, babe," I said. I looked quickly and awkwardly at August's birth mother and her parents, hoping something would happen to change the subject. When nothing did, I looked back at Tru and said, "We can talk about that later."

Thankfully, Truly did not press us to continue the conversation.

For the next few days, Josh and I both noticed Truly's behavior was off. When we had a moment to think things through rationally, we both agreed that her off behavior was triggered by the visit with August's birth mother. We decided we needed to reconsider the way we interacted as a family with August's and Macyn's birth families. We were going to have to guard Truly's heart in this matter for as long as she needed us to.

The next time August's birth mother reached out to see him, we set things up so that Truly would not be there, nor would she know about the meeting. We didn't want to be sneaky or leave her out, but we did know we had entered a new space with Truly and her adoption story. And for the time being, if we could protect her six-year-old heart, we would.

Our kids have created some pretty tense situations for us. Not one IEP meeting has gone by in which we did not have to sit in the tension of us believing one thing is best for Macyn and the educators in the room believing another. And there's no way to sit across from the woman who gave birth to your child and not feel all kinds of tension. And when you sit across the table from someone of a different race and try to understand the ways they see the world and the ways the world sees them, things are likely going to get tense.

But let's not continue believing that tension is all bad. If we want to understand the fullness of God, and if we want to have healthy and whole relationships, then we need to learn to sit in the tension. We need to enter into dialogues and relationships with people who are different from us and allow tension to make us stronger and more loving.

Being around people who are different from us is hard. Most people I know, including myself, have a knee-jerk reaction of avoiding tension at all costs. When we make an intentional choice to live outside of our comfort zones, we will likely soon find ourselves in the center of tension. And when that happens,

> We need to enter into dialogues and relationships with people who are different from us and allow tension to make us stronger and more loving.

let's take a deep breath and just sit. Let's remember how Jesus spent so much of his time on earth sitting in uncomfortable situations, bringing together people who disagreed strongly with one another.

Yes, when we try to understand someone else's world, we will experience more tension than we'd like. But I believe that when we put ourselves aside for the sake of someone else, we find Jesus. And if we sit in the tension rather than try to avoid it or pray it away, we can begin to build the bridges we need to heal our lives, restore our relationships, and rebuild a busted-up world.

Chapter 12

LISTEN, LEARN, AND LOVE

We have a lot of sayings in the Avis home—mantras and chants to get us through the day or out the door or up off the sidewalk. The mantras vary from child to child.

Because August is so little and his speech is still developing, we often ask him to respond with a thumbs-up or an "okay!" And as the prince of the household, August has led us to develop a few mantras whose purpose is mainly to remind him that the world does not in fact revolve around him, such as, "You need to be kind and helpful." To which he is supposed to respond with a thumbs-up or an "okay!" but sometimes responds instead with an "I don't want to."

The greatest lie Macyn tells herself is, "I can't do it." For most of the tasks in front of her, she feels defeated before she even begins. So, we have her repeat back to us phrases such as, "I am brave," or "I can do it!" When she's feeling especially challenged or uncertain, our conversations usually go something like this:

Me: "Macyn, what do Avises do?"
Macyn: "We do hard things."
Me: "That's right! You can do it! Say it back to me."
Macyn: "I can do it!"
Me: "That's right! Now, do it!"

This little back-and-forth between Macyn and me doesn't always result in her actually doing the difficult task before her, but it really does help her approach a situation with a little more confidence. We aren't sure where her lack of confidence comes from, but if a person wants to be in Macyn's life, it is a nonnegotiable requirement to believe in her. The truth that she is brave and can do hard things is a truth we want to seed deep in her heart, mind, and soul.

With Truly, the mantras and conversations are quite different. Truly has zero issue with confidence. Truly believes she can do anything she darn well pleases. I love this aspect of Truly's personality. I was not a confident child, and I always wished I had been. Believe me when I say that I'm thankful she has the confidence she does, and I pray she never loses it.

I'm also aware that, as a Caucasian mama raising a child of color, I will never fully understand Truly's reality or how she is perceived in the world. When Truly steps into the world with confidence and authority, the systemic racism that wouldn't think twice about such qualities in me may have little grace for Truly. The color of my skin has always given me advantages that Truly does not have. No matter how hard I work to be a listener and learner in this area, aspects of my privilege can be a blind spot for me. So my job here as Truly's mom is to be aware of this blind spot and to celebrate and affirm Truly's confidence whenever I can.

I love watching Truly's confidence show up in simple ways, such as when we're out in public and she needs to find a bathroom or even order her own food from a menu. She has a confident authority about her, with the power to get what she wants. Still, she is young, and all day every day, she seems to want pretty much everything, especially all the things she's not supposed to have—such as screen time, candy, cookies, cotton candy, soda, more screen time, and more sugar. Most nights, Josh and I have crashed on the couch after a long day, one of us saying to the other, "What will eventually serve her well when she's an adult may just about do us in while she's seven." Lord, have mercy! Raising world changers is exhausting.

Coupled with her confidence is her strong resistance to being taught. Truly knows just about everything there is to know about everything in all of life and the history of the world. Even her question asking is done with a surprising, and slightly infuriating, level of certainty.

> **Truly:** "Hey, Mom, when you were six, what was your favorite food?"
>
> **Me:** "I liked most foods, but I really loved to eat cream cheese and olive sandwiches."
>
> **Truly (before I get the whole sentence out):** "Oh, yeah, I already knew that!"
>
> **Me:** "How could you know that if I am just now telling you for the first time?"

Truly: "Because I just knew."
Me: "No, Truly. No, you didn't."

At which point she'll want to argue about what she already knew. If I am feeling feisty—or foolish—I will let this back-and-forth about how she believes she is right but I know she is wrong go on longer than I'd like to admit.

In addition to her confidence in knowing everything, or maybe because of it, Truly is the kind of kid who also wants to do all the things and believes she *can* do all the things with ease and excellence. Then when she realizes she will have to practice and work hard to attain certain skills, she's out. Recently, she decided she wanted to play guitar. This decision was based on the Disney movie *Coco*, in which the main character, a boy roughly her age, picks up a guitar and plays it like a professional. After watching this movie, Truly was certain she should and could do that too.

Both of my parents are professional musicians, and my mom plays the guitar, so as soon as Truly showed an interest in learning to play, my parents were thrilled. For Christmas, they got her a student guitar, and shortly thereafter we set her up with lessons. It didn't take Truly long to discover she is not a Disney character and cannot simply pick up a guitar and make meaningful music. And she was gravely disappointed when after her first and second lessons, she was still not a professional guitar player.

My parents, Josh, the guitar teacher, and I have all explained to Truly how she'll need to practice every single day if she wants to learn how to play the guitar. We've told her she will be able to play more and more music, but it starts with learning one chord at a time and practicing that one chord over and over and over again until her fingers and her brain make a connection to the chord and it becomes a natural movement. But Truly doesn't want to hear this. And so every day when I tell her it's time to practice, she whines and complains. All of a sudden, her legs get weak and give out from under her and she is a pile on the floor.

And this behavior is not limited to playing the guitar. Truly has a desire to try her hand at many different sports and art forms, and as soon as she realizes she cannot perform the task at the level of a professional, she wants to quit. When I sit down to talk with her about the value of hard work and discipline and how everyone who is great at a skill started where she is and had to practice over and over again, she always interrupts me with, "I know that, Mom." I know, she's only seven years old, but gosh, for a seven-year-old she sure does know a lot!

If I'm being totally honest, and we all know I can't help but be, I'm not so different from my Truly. When it comes to learning a new skill, the greatest difference between Truly and me is that she is far more talented than I will ever be. When I was a kid, I took piano lessons, flute lessons, and guitar lessons, and I resented the amount of time and discipline it would take for me to play any of those instruments well. And I eventually quit every one of them.

Even in my motherhood, I started out stubbornly resistant to learning how to be the kind of mom my kids needed. When Truly came along, I parented her just as I had parented Macyn, and when it didn't work, I became frustrated at her, not recognizing it was my own lack of learning that was making mothering her difficult for me.

Truly's dad and I keep hoping she finds the one thing she is passionate about, the one thing she won't quit. We are trusting that, in the process, she will become passionate about the art of learning as well, or at least she'll appreciate the fact that it's a good thing to want to learn.

Which brings us to the mantra we find ourselves using with our Truly Star: "Be a listener, a learner, and a lover." We say this to all of the children as well as to each other, but it was inspired by our Truly. So while we tell Macyn over and over again that Avises do hard things, we tell Truly over and over again that Avises are listeners, learners, and lovers.

This mantra, this lesson, is one I revisit often. It's easy for me to see the need for my children to become listeners, learners, and lovers, but I sometimes have blinders on when it comes to applying this mantra in my own life. Becoming a listener, learner, and lover can be really hard work. Honestly, sometimes I just prefer to sit in my echo chamber, enjoying all the ways I'm affirmed for how right and smart and funny I am. It's easier to stay in that place. But at the end of the day, I want a better world for my kids. I want a better world for myself. I want a better world for all of us—and I'm discovering that the only way to realize this better world is to love all the people more. And the way to more love is to make a conscious effort to be a listener and a learner. It's a package deal.

When we decide to be listeners and learners, there are generally two ways to approach it: we can focus on what we gain for ourselves, or we can focus on how we can help others. If you stop to really think about it, learning tends to lean toward serving our own self-interests. We pursue a degree or take a class to master a body of knowledge or learn a skill because it's something we want to do, want to be good at, or want to understand for ourselves. In the process, we also want to feel good about ourselves. These are all good reasons to want to learn.

> The way to more love is to make a conscious effort to be a listener and a learner.

But we can also learn for reasons that go beyond ourselves. For example, we can learn about a specific person or people group in order to deepen our understanding, recognizing that understanding this person or group better can lead to healing and relationship and positive change. For example, a person may take a class to learn all she can about Down syndrome for the sake of having that knowledge or for the sake of working with people who have Down syndrome. Or a person may meet Macyn and August and then go online to learn all she can about Down syndrome so she can have a better understanding of—and therefore a meaningful relationship with—Macyn and August.

Just as we tend to approach learning in either self-focused or others-focused ways, there are two ways that people tend to approach listening. The first and most common is listening in order to speak. That's when we listen just long enough to make our own point or to prove someone else's point wrong. I confess I'm often guilty of this kind of listening, of waiting for my turn to speak only so I can let the person talking know how wrong he is and how right I am or, if we do agree on the topic, how much I know about it.

Then there's the second way to approach listening, which is true and meaningful listening. This is when we listen deeply to gain understanding of the speaker. I love this challenge from author and activist Terry Tempest Williams, "Can we listen with our whole beings, not just our minds, and offer our attention rather than our opinions?"[7] This kind of listening is needed for true understanding. But I fear it is sadly lacking in our world today.

Let's look back in time at the 2016 United States presidential election as an example. Do you remember that election? Or rather, how could we forget? I remember it took just one hot second of scrolling through Facebook for me to feel shocked and appalled by the hateful, hurtful things people felt at liberty to post. Even men and women who claim to love Jesus said unthinkable things about others who are created in God's image. It seemed as if people were sitting behind their digital devices just waiting for an opportunity to put others down and prove themselves. It seemed as if every American decided that only *their* reality and *their* opinions and *their* stories mattered. It seemed as if a new kind of wedge was pounded into the bedrock of our society, and the front end of the wedge was our inability to truly listen to one another. Can I get an *oy vey*?

Maybe it's because I no longer wear the rose-colored lenses through which I once viewed life, but it seems as if, now more than ever, people are choosing to talk rather than listen, teach rather than learn, and claim self-righteousness rather than love others. Friends, humanity is broken and hurting because of it.

And I think it's safe to say, if humanity is broken and hurting, so is God.

When I consider all the voices shouting about how right they are and how wrong everyone else is, I wonder what would happen if we stopped shouting long enough to listen, and set aside our pride long enough to learn from the person speaking—to listen and learn for the sake of understanding. What if we did as Terry Tempest Williams suggests and offered our attention rather than our opinions?

Honestly, the self-centered, self-righteous, and self-important nature of our communications on the national level often reminds me of the many conversations we've had with Truly when we ask her to be a listener, a learner, and a lover. I look at how much more listening, learning, and loving our nation needs to do, and I worry that our society is heading toward becoming a know-it-all seven-year-old.

Sometimes when Truly is so dead set on being right and being heard—to the point that she is unable to learn and listen—it's because she is, in fact, right. Sometimes people with strong moral convictions believe that if they listen to, learn from, and love someone with whom they disagree—morally, politically, or otherwise—they are in some way approving of that person's views or choices. So, let's be clear here. Being a listener, a learner, and a lover does not mean we compromise our faith, our passions, or our convictions. It does not mean we have to agree with one another. But it does mean we have to make some space for one another.

It was Jesus who told us to not only love our neighbors—those with whom we agree—but also to love our enemies.

It's important to recognize that our enemies are not some "bad guys" on the other side of the globe but may in fact be the people who voted differently than we did. Our enemy may be the person who lives a different lifestyle than we do. According to Jesus, these are the very people we must love—and how can we love them if we're not willing to listen to them and learn from them? When was the last time you felt loved by someone who refused to listen to you?

When we make space in our lives to listen and learn, we make space in our lives to love. We allow ourselves to engage with the world, not as a seven-year-old who already knows everything, but as listeners and learners and lovers who believe that everyone is valuable enough to be heard. Much of the time, love simply looks like listening. And love will lead us toward understanding. When we have understanding, we can more easily drop our pointing fingers and extend a hand of welcome. When we have understanding, we can release our cynical spirit, listen to one another with humility and grace, and learn from each other's realities. And even if we wholeheartedly disagree, we can find a way to embrace one another in love.

Chapter 13

CHOOSE CIRCLES
OVER LINES

Macyn's grandparents got her a giant trampoline for her sixth birthday. The night before her big day, after the kids were tucked away safely in their beds, Josh and I rolled out all the pieces and put together that giant round trampoline and its net enclosure pole by pole and spring by spring—and then we filled it up with balloons. When our birthday girl woke up the next morning, she ran into the backyard, climbed up onto the trampoline, and jumped until she could jump no more.

A few months later, when our landlords told us they would no longer be renting their home and we'd have to move, my first thought was that trampoline. I thought about the hours it took to put it together and the hours it would take to take it apart and the hours it would take to put it together again. But that's what we did. Once we moved into our new home, we rolled out all the pieces and put the trampoline back together pole by pole and spring by spring.

One year later, our new landlord called to let us know he had sold the house to his nephew and we'd have to move. *Ugh!* We couldn't believe it. This would be our third move in three years. And the first thing I thought about, once again, was having to disassemble and reassemble that dang trampoline.

Fortunately, we ended up finding another rental only three blocks away. Unfortunately, however, this rental was a small backhouse with an even smaller patio, and there was no way the trampoline would fit. Because the kids used the trampoline all the time, we couldn't imagine packing it up and letting it sit in a garage, so I got an idea.

Our new rental was only six houses down from some of our dearest friends, Katie and Danny. They had a yard, and, as a bonus, they lived directly across the street from Macyn's elementary school. So I proposed to them that we put the trampoline in their yard and that we get it to their house by laying it on its side and rolling it so we wouldn't have to break it down and put it back together again. They agreed this was an excellent plan, and so the week we moved, Josh and another friend hoisted the trampoline over the fence in our backyard; set it on its side; rolled it up the street, around the corner and down the next street; and then hoisted it over Katie and Danny's fence and into their backyard.

Here's the coolest part. When we moved our trampoline to Katie and Danny's yard, we had no idea the positive relational impact it would have on Macyn. You see, the trampoline could be seen from the crosswalk in front of the school, and when kids saw Macyn, Truly, and August jumping, they asked if they could join. It was slow at first, with just a couple of girls who knew Macyn asking if they could join in on the jumping fun. Then they told their friends, who told their friends, and on any given Monday through Friday afternoon, Macyn was circled up on the trampoline with a variety of kids from her school.

While the kids jumped, I sat and watched, occasionally stepping in to make sure August didn't get trampled. Over time, though, the kids themselves just seemed to know how to create space for August or the other little sisters or brothers who joined in, so that everyone could enjoy the trampoline experience at their own level. When the atmosphere on the trampoline became overwhelming for August, Macyn, or another child, one of the kids would stop jumping and somehow get the rest of the kids to stop as well. Then they'd circle up and sit around the perimeter, and each take turns doing some kind of awesome jump one at a time.

Occasionally, though, there were moments when the jumping and flipping kids took zero notice of the ones struggling to make it amid the bouncing chaos, and I had to intervene and encourage them to circle up and allow everyone a chance to enjoy the trampoline. But whether they did it on their own or at my prompting, every time they sat in that circle, they were naturally able to take notice of each other and then jump in a way that worked for the group as a whole.

I'm not sure this would have happened if the trampoline had been a rectangle or a square. Imagine the kids sitting not in a circle but in a line. There would probably have been confusion about what was going on in the front or the back or the middle. If the kid in the back needed everyone to stop jumping for a second, it would have been challenging for the kid in the front to know that, and because the kid in the front couldn't see the kid in the back, there would be little reason for the front kid to even care about the back kid.

The circle is a powerful shape. It is a universal symbol of wholeness. And there's a reason for that. It can build understanding and a sense of community that goes far beyond our backyard trampoline.

In many Native American traditions, the circle is a symbol of equality, where no person is more prominent than any other. When gathering in a circle, there's an understanding that all people are allowed to speak and that their words will be accepted and respected on an equal basis. Luther Standing Bear of the Oglala Sioux, a notable author, educator, philosopher, and actor, says, "Love settles within the circle, embracing it and thereby lasting forever, turning within itself."[8]

> When gathering in a circle, there's an understanding that all people are allowed to speak and that their words will be accepted and respected on an equal basis.

I love the idea that love exists within a circle rather than being boxed up or confined by rigid lines. When I read Luther Standing Bear's words, I envision our family's daily morning prayers in which we take a few moments to circle up, hold hands, and look at one another face-to-face. Even when our prayer is done and we let go of each other's hands to head our separate ways, we take this circle of everlasting love with us.

Circles stand in stark contrast to lines. Lines create boundaries around or within an object. Lines separate and divide.

Think of the last time you had to stand in a long line—what emotion does that memory evoke? I'm guessing it's a nega-tive emotion, which is why so many of us do our level best to avoid lines.

More importantly, when we stand in a line, we rarely turn around to see who's standing behind us, which means we have little opportunity to know anything about the people in front of us and even less about the people in line behind us. Lines can also be indicators of worth or privilege—those at the front of a line being superior and those at the back of a line being inferior. Lines, by design, have a beginning and an end, a first and a last, a hierarchy. And wherever the line is made up of people, whoever is first inevitably has the power and the privilege.

While these observations about circles and lines may seem simple, I've experienced the not-so-simple ways they show up in the complex systems that govern most aspects of our lives—systems such as our schools, workplaces, and even our neighborhoods and communities. Most of these systems are "line" systems—they work in favor of the kinds of people who have the abilities and the resources to make it to the front of the line. But they don't work for those without abilities and resources—those who are dependent on the community and require the relationships and love of circle systems.

But let's not forget that it's often the people at the front of the line, the people the systems favor, who have the greatest need to circle up and be known. The space at the front of the line creates isolation and misunderstanding. But when we are accustomed to front-of-line benefits, we don't want to give that up; we don't want to risk our power, our place, and our privilege. But if those of us at the front of the line are brave enough, we may just find that when we bend and flex until the line becomes a circle, isolation is replaced with community.

In his book *Becoming Human*, my hero Jean Vanier points out how difficult and uncomfortable it can be to even take notice of people who are different, the people who are most likely to be pushed to the back of the line: "Who are those who are different? . . . Often, they are in discomfort while others live in comfort. Their cries become dangerous for those of us who live in comfort. If we listen to their cries and open up our hearts, it will cost us something. So we pretend not to hear the cry and so exclude them."[9]

To this I would add, not only do we pretend not to hear their cries, but we also situate ourselves so far from their cries that we no longer have to pretend not to hear them because we truly cannot. We make our way as far up the line as we can to place ourselves as far out of earshot as we can from the cries of anyone who is different.

Our efforts to have Macyn fully included in a general education classroom and be seen as a valuable and worthy member of her school is a story about lines over circles. When we questioned the lines that had been put in place—specifically, the lines that separated her from the general ed classroom—it was both an inconvenience and a threat. We were asking everyone involved to rethink the structure of how the whole system is set up, and we were asking the people who benefited most from these systems to lay down their power—and to see that in so doing, they were not giving up any of their rights, but rather extending those same rights to others.

When we said we wanted our daughter out of the special education classroom and fully included in her school community, we were creating a space for all the people in the school to hear her cries. We believed that as those in power circled up and then widened the circle to create a space for Macyn within it, they could begin to see the power in her. By insisting that our daughter not be placed in a segregated classroom, we placed a spotlight on some of the unjust realities of this system. Although the education system claims to be set up for all children, it only works for those who have always had access to the front of the line or to the rare students capable of pushing their way to the front. When we challenged the school to circle up, we asked it to take on a shape that allows my daughter's face to be visible to everyone in the space. It was a simple enough request, but it wasn't easy.

And the need to circle up—to hand over our power— does not begin or end in our schools. We need to start choosing circles over lines in the majority of our societal systems. Although there may be a time and place for lines, I wonder what could happen if we as a culture began to imagine and work toward a world in which the lines that shape us can be bent toward one another. If we begin to bend, I believe these bent lines will turn to circles, until we finally see each other face-to-face.

Of course, often there's little reason for people who stand at the front of the lines to want to turn around and see those standing way behind them. Why would those of us who benefit from the lines want to make a change to circles? Jean Vanier tackles this question in *Becoming Human*:

> The excluded, I believe, live certain values that we all need to discover and to live ourselves before we can become truly human . . . If we start to include the disadvantaged in our lives and enter into heartfelt relationships with them, they will change things in us. They will call us to be people of mutual trust, to take time to listen and be with each other. They will call us out from our individualism and need for power into belonging to each other and being open to others. They will break down the prejudices and protective walls that gave rise to exclusion in the first place. They will then start to affect our human organizations, revealing new ways of being and walking together.[10]

The reason we choose to give up our power and gather together in circles is so we can know each other and be known. It's only then that we become truly human.

Choosing to embrace the challenges and graces of doing life in circles has drastically and irrevocably shaped me as a human and as a mother. More often than not, it is my kids who are the ones at the back of the lines in the systems they have to navigate. The more my kids have pushed me to turn around and see those at the back of the line, the more I believe in the power of the circle-up mentality.

I've made it my calling to create a world of circles for my kids, but it's a calling that runs even deeper than that. It is within circles—spaces in which all people can be seen and find worth and belonging—that I have experienced Jesus in new ways, and learned to see all the people he loves, face-to-face. I see Jesus when I shift my gaze and my heart from my own successes and seek out and cherish the differences in the people around me. As I learn to see everyone as my equal, I recognize Jesus as our great equalizer. The circle is a symbol of equality, where no person is more prominent than any other. If I teach my kids how to see Jesus in others and how to gather together all kinds of people to know and share God's love, then as a mother I can say, "It is well with my soul."

> The reason we choose to give up our power and gather together in circles is so we can know each other and be known.

Choosing circles over lines is a mind-set that takes intentionality and time to develop. Just as the kids on the trampoline had to pause their jumping chaos long enough to notice each other, we will need to look for places in our lives where we're so focused on ourselves that we fail to see the people around us who are at risk of being trampled. We need to stop jumping long enough to notice the people who also need a turn. And just as the kids on the trampoline made a conscious effort to stop and circle up, we too need to step out of our place in line and begin to use the resources around us to create a circle where everyone is seen and cherished, and no one person is more deserving than any other. And it is then that we can know what it means to be fully human.

Chapter 14

LET'S TALK RACE

A couple of years ago, I stood in an old barn on a small farm in Iowa. It was a hot and muggy July day, and I was there with my whole extended family. I've been visiting Iowa my entire life, and for the past decade or so, my grandma has brought all her kids, grandkids, and great-grandkids to her home in Middletown, Iowa, to be together over the Fourth of July weekend. We gather together from California, Florida, and New York, so each time we city folk visit, we tour a farm and entertain ourselves with farm living.

We were in the hot, muggy barn to see the cows. While our small kids ran around, jumped on bales of hay, and stuck out their hands toward the timid cows to try to convince them to come closer, the farmer began explaining the history of the barn. "This barn used to be a part of the underground railroad," he said. "They used to hide slaves in here who were making their way to freedom."

His history lesson stopped me in my tracks, and I let out a small gasp. I stood staring up at the beams, feeling the heavy air, looking at my feet on the ground, and I tried to imagine the souls whose feet had stood here before me, finding refuge in this place as they ran for their freedom and their lives. As I watched my kids jump and play, I tried to imagine a mother, perhaps my age, holding her children close, hushing them as they began to fidget. Or the mother who stood here childless, her children wrested from her arms and sold as property. I thought about all the heroes who had been under the roof of this old barn, risking their lives for the freedom that should have been theirs all along—a freedom violently ripped from them because of their dark skin. And I thought about all the people, including myself, who were there to see the cows, when the true importance of the place was found in its sacred history.

It was on that night, July 5, 2016, that Alton Sterling, a black man selling CDs outside a convenience store in Baton Rouge, Louisiana, was shot and killed by police. By the time I woke up the next morning and heard the news, social media was full of rage and judgment from all sides, mostly in the form of hashtags: #blacklivesmatter, #alllivesmatter, #bluelivesmatter, #nojusticenopeace.

As I read the news reports, I'm embarrassed to admit I went looking for evidence that Sterling's poor choices had led to his death. I wanted to say, "See? He had a gun in his back pocket," and "See? He didn't pay attention to the cop's demands." I wanted to believe it had nothing to do with the color of his skin. I think my whiteness and my privileged life had programmed me to think that way. Work hard enough and make good choices, and you'll be just fine, right? But prior to this event, prior to the reporting and social media uproar, prior to reports of a whole string of black men and women being shot by police, I had made a choice to have relationships with people who are different from me, including black men and women.

I had been wrestling with racial injustice as my African American friends helped me recognize it and invited me to talk less and listen more. And in so doing, I could finally hear their broken hearts, which had been crushed by the pernicious legacy of slavery. As I did life alongside black men and women, I was learning that their experiences with racial discrimination were real and valid and that systemic racism, established by slavery hundreds of years ago, is not "fake news" and has not been eradicated.

As I scrolled through social media and news reports on my phone, trying to find a reason that it may have been acceptable for police to shoot and kill Alton Sterling, I was able to pause, remembering how little I actually understood about how systemic racism affects black men like Alton and white women like me. I stopped looking to be justified, because I remembered how much more I still had to learn.

What I was learning was that until we deal with the systemic racism rampant in our society, it won't make much difference if men like Alton Sterling make good choices or not. Black men and women continue to face negative consequences

> *I stopped looking to be justified, because I remembered how much more I still had to learn.*

in our society simply because of the color of their skin. I also knew it *would* matter if I chose to remain silent and not engage in this conversation—a conversation I could easily choose to skip out on or ignore because, really, systemic racism does not negatively affect people like me with white skin. The fact that people of color can never choose to ignore systemic racism while simultaneously being oppressed by it, and that white people *can* choose to ignore systemic racism while simultaneously benefiting from it, is the very reason people with white skin—and especially people with white skin who love Jesus—need to acknowledge the injustices of systemic racism, join the conversation, and engage in the work of reconciliation.

And you know what? So much of me would rather sit in silent judgment and misunderstanding. Or just sit silently while understanding full well. It's just a lot easier to do so. Even now, I have moments when I wish I could ignore or, worse yet, try to rationalize the structures of racism in our nation. Even the fact that I have the option of sitting it out is an expression of white privilege.

But God keeps stretching me and showing me how every single person is created in the image of God, and that means I can only know God fully if I try to know all the people created in his image. I can only begin to imagine how God's heart breaks for those who are suffering at the hands of broken systems. It was God's grace bestowed on me when my children—two of whom have Down syndrome and one of whom is African American and Guatemalan—enabled me to see these broken systems more clearly and to feel their impact more personally. Unfortunately, we tend to not act on issues of injustice until they do affect us personally.

Yes, it's easier to sit in the places we feel comfortable. To surround ourselves with people with whom we see eye to eye.

And though there is a time and a place for being with those who are just like us, I wonder if those of us with pale skin are so used to taking up the entire bench that we don't even notice all of those who've never been invited to take a seat. My friendships with people of color have allowed me to see that not only does everyone not have a seat on the bench, but I am taking up more than my fair share of seats!

This conversation of race is one of the most uncomfortable I have ever chosen to step into. As a white mama raising a child of color, it is a necessary discomfort and a conversation I feel responsible to take part in. A lot of the discomfort comes from my lack of knowledge and experience, which only makes it all the more important for me to engage it as a listener and a learner. The less I understand and can relate to a person's reality, the more I need to learn from that person.

The deeper I get into racial issues and the more I make space to understand the role I'm called to play in reconciliation, the more I feel the urge to inch my way out. But God's gracious gift of Truly Star in my life has taken away that option. So I continue to learn all I can and to further my understanding.

My friend John, who runs racial reconciliation workshops, recommended a podcast called *Scene on Radio* in which the host, John Biewen, explores the human experience and American society. In 2017, Biewen, a white man, invited a cohost named Chenjerai Kumanyika, a black man and scholar, to help him navigate a fourteen-episode series titled *Seeing White*. The focus of the series was to talk about today's racial turbulence by looking at white people as a group and by exploring, historically, what it means to be white. I cannot recommend this series enough. Yet, in total honesty, as a white person listening to it, there were many moments when I wanted to turn it off and go back to sitting in my comfortable, ignorant space.

Biewen and Kumanyika begin by going all the way back to a time when race wasn't even a thing and when the notion of race was invented and who invented it. Then they step into the years of slavery, identifying where it started and how it ended up in the United States. With each significant historical and scientific event they identified and unpacked, I wanted to crawl out of my white skin.

Toward the end of the series, as the two men discussed what they had learned about the history of whiteness, Kumanyika asks his cohost and all of us listening a question that still haunts me: "When was whiteness good?" At which point there was a long pause, because the question was rhetorical. Biewen knew, after all the research he and Kumanyika had done for the series, that the answer is, "It never was." Kumanyika goes on to say, "If you identify that way, I don't envy you in terms of having to try to think about what that means."

This has been a tension for me as I've tried to be a bridge builder and raise my daughter who is African American and Guatemalan and whose skin is darker than my own. It's the tension of living in a society that views my whiteness as a good thing, while simultaneously trying to be in communities with people of color who see whiteness as a threat to the well-being of their ethnic identity and their day-to-day safety. And it's the tension of feeling humiliated about what my whiteness represents and also knowing that I am created by God, with pleasure and intention, to have the ethnic identity I do and the skin color I do, and that I shouldn't feel bad about this. These are tensions I'm still learning to navigate. It's not about viewing whiteness as good or bad, but rather acknowledging the sins of our white past and how those sins continue to be active in our present, and then doing the hard work to secure an equitable future for everyone.

This fact that the color of one's skin has positive or negative repercussions on our day-to-day living is not a theoretical reality for me. It shows up in real ways, even in places as seemingly innocent as the toys my children play with. Let me give you an example: Truly got a white Barbie doll for her seventh birthday. If you think this sounds like a loaded sentence, you're right.

I have always been mindful of the toys my kids play with, not so much for their usefulness or educational value but for the subtle messages they can communicate to my children. When Macyn came home with us, even though she has light-colored skin, we were intentional in making sure her books and toys represented different kinds of people.

Early on, as a mother of a daughter, I confess I was anti-Barbie. Barbie feels like an insufferably high standard to aspire to. Her long lean limbs and silky, straight blonde hair sets the beauty bar at an impossibly high height. Not to mention the fact that most of her outfits are ones I pray my teenage daughters never wear. I was convinced if I allowed my daughter to play with Barbies, she would get the message, even if subtly, that she needed to meet Barbie's impossible beauty standards. Plus, Mattel does not make a Barbie doll with Down syndrome, so there is that. Did I overthink it? Likely. As it has been with basically every aspect of my parenting, I have shifted, adjusted, and, let's be honest here, lightened up over the years. Still, I've never bought my children Barbie dolls.

A few years ago around Christmas time, I saw some generic-brand Barbie-like dolls that had dark skin and dark curly hair. Their outfits were still questionable, but you can't win them all, so I purchased two of them—one for Macyn and one for Truly. Truly was thankful for the toy but did not share the same appreciation I did that the doll resembled her. She let me know she still wanted a "real" Barbie.

When the grandparents and aunties ask for gift ideas for the kids, I typically send them a dozen or more links to books with characters who are not Caucasian, characters who portray powerful women, or, when I'm lucky enough to find one, characters who have a different ability. I'm pretty sure my family rolls their eyes from time to time when receiving these lists, wondering when I will lighten up and not take this whole toy and children's book thing so seriously. Anyway . . .

A few weeks before Truly's seventh birthday, I got a message from one of her grandparents letting me know they had been looking online at the toys Truly had included on her birthday wish list. On the top of the list was a Barbie and a Barbie dream house. "Would it be okay to buy these gifts for Truly?" the grandparent asked. I said no to the dream house because we have no space in our small house for another small house. And then I said okay to the Barbie, thinking I've been way too uptight in my anti-Barbie ways. It's just a doll, and, let's be real here, I have greater battles to fight than the diversity of my children's dolls. Or so I thought.

Well, as you might guess, Truly did get a Barbie, a doll with white skin and long, shiny, straight blonde hair. While it was not my favorite toy, I convinced myself it really should not be that big of a deal. Until . . .

The morning after she got her new Barbie, Truly came into my room with a white dress from her closet I had never seen her wear.

"Can I cut this right here?" she pointed to the waistline of the dress.

"Uh, I don't think so, babe. Why in the world do you want to cut that dress?"

"I'm trying to match my Barbie."

"Oh, honey," I said as I pulled her in and kissed her on top of the head, "we aren't cutting our clothes. Find something else you can wear that you won't have to cut."

She gave a big sigh and rolled her eyes and stomped out of the room as only a seven-year-old teenager can. Because you know, being told you cannot cut your clothes is such a bummer.

A few minutes later, she came back into the room with a solution that satisfied us both—she had the dress tucked into a denim miniskirt.

"Nice solution, Tru! You look great."

Tru held up her Barbie doll and looked at herself in the full-length mirror in my room. "Mom, how can I get my hair straight?"

"Well, babe, you have curly hair, so your hair is curly *and* gorgeous." This was not the first time we'd had this conversation, so I wasn't planning on getting into it with her.

"But, Mom, can you just please use that thing to straighten my hair? Please? Please? Please?"

"You mean the flatiron?"

Truly nodded.

"Nope. We are not going to straighten your hair, Tru. Not today."

"Ugh! Mom! This is so not fair." Truly stomped her dramatic little feet and raised her voice. "I JUST WANT TO LOOK LIKE MY BARBIE!"

I had to take a deep breath because I was fuming. I hated how a doll had created this moment in our home. I wanted to take that skinny blonde Barbie doll, cut off her silky straight hair, and toss her in the trash. But mostly I wanted to cry and scoop up my perfectly-made-just-as-she-is daughter and take her away from the things in the world that tell her she is not enough simply because of the color of her skin and the texture of her hair. And the kicker, the punch to the gut? I am a white woman with straight hair, and I will never be able to fully understand her reality, and that left me feeling helpless and sad.

My husband and I are intentional about trying to understand how the color of our skin offers us advantages, and how those advantages perpetuate narratives that make little girls with dark skin and curly hair wish they looked more like Barbie. Because we are aware of this and are desperate to change these negative narratives, we are intentional about the toys our kids play with, the books they read, and the shows they watch, making sure they represent all kinds of different people. While Truly's fixation with looking like her white Barbie doll is not coming from us, it *is* coming from the racial bias embedded in our culture. There is only so much protecting and planning and avoiding we can do before she has a desire to have straight hair and light skin. The fact that we, her white family, have those traits does not help in her narrative. This breaks my heart and fuels that feeling of helplessness. In addition, it creates an urgency in me to recognize the blind spots I have because of the privileges given to me by my white skin and to do all I can to shed light on these blind spots in the wider culture so I can better help Truly navigate this world.

Here's the other thing. My experience with Truly is just a drop in a much larger bucket. The problem of little black girls wanting to look like white dolls, white characters, or white movie stars is one my African American friends with daughters have been battling for a long time already. They've shared many similar stories of their daughters wanting to be like the Disney princesses who are white or being drawn only to white Barbie dolls. Knowing that deep seeds of racial bias are negatively affecting how children of different ethnicities see themselves, even when being raised by and surrounded by people who look like them, only heightens my awareness of how intentional we need to be as we raise Truly.

Don't get me wrong. Barbie is not all bad. Though I have strong convictions for my own reasons, it doesn't mean everyone has to ban Barbie. You and your kids love Barbie? There's no shame in that game. You do you, friend! But there is something deeper here, beyond whether or not Barbie is good for our kids. And the more that societal norms play in our favor, the more difficult it is to see the deeper thing happening. I know that for me the advantages I have as a white person—including something as simple as the norms in the doll world always mirroring my appearance—can make it extremely difficult to see past my reality to the reality of someone such as my daughter Truly.

Being Truly's mom has helped me notice many of the blind spots—in my own life and in the broader culture—that work against creating an inclusive and equitable world. And when the systems favor my middle-class, able-bodied, white-skinned self, there is great risk for blinders to subtly creep back into my line of vision. In other words—and at the very least here, friends—it's worth noting and remembering that our culture, whether in subtle or obvious ways, does not love and include all kinds of people equally. And this message is often spread in sneaky ways that we need to call out and be aware of when we make choices for our kids and for ourselves.

When I reflect back to that day on the farm in Iowa, I realize it mattered to me that the barn was much more than a place to house the cows only because some of the blinders in my life had been removed. The importance of the history of the barn—that it had been a part of the underground railroad—weighed on me due largely to the fact that I had taken the time to listen to and learn from the people in my life who are African American, to hear their stories and sit in some uncomfortable truths. Namely, that the brutal history of the United States of America is still so deeply rooted and active in our systems today that some of us continue to benefit because of it while others continue to suffer because of it. Being an intentional listener and learner in this difficult conversation about race has helped me embrace these truths and own the blind spots in my life so I can seek to make the changes I need to make to create a better world for my Truly and for all of humanity.

Conversations about race and racial injustice, as well as joining the efforts in eradicating racial injustice, are so incredibly difficult, and are so important to God. God loves all of us so much, and he created us to live in harmony with one another, making these incredibly difficult tasks incredibly worthy as well. I know that for me these conversations are intense, humbling, and often painful, but I keep on showing up because these are the very places God hangs out. When we choose to engage in difficult conversations about race, I believe God is there, just waiting for us to gain a better understanding of each other, which will help us develop a better understanding of God. God lingers in these uncomfortable spaces to be with us as we feel the weight of it all, as we recognize that when anyone created in the image of God is hurting, all of us are hurting. And as we come to a better understanding of this truth, as we enter into these conversations and spaces and do our part in building bridges and making space for others, we will discover that it is not only uncomfortable and hard, but it is also holy and good. We will discover we have an opportunity here to not only know each other better, but to better know the heart of God.

Chapter 15

OWN YOUR
INFLUENCE

From time to time, I'm fortunate enough to find myself in my car on a Sunday afternoon when my local public radio station airs one of my very favorite shows, *The Moth Radio Hour*. For more than twenty years, *The Moth* has been devoted to the art and craft of storytelling, believing that stories have the ability to connect humanity. *The Moth* holds events around the country where people can tell a true story—live and without notes. If I arrive at my destination while I'm in the middle of listening to a story, I will sit in the car and wait for the story to come to an end. No matter the topic, I always feel captivated by every word, even if the story is nothing I can relate to. Whether it's a story about someone's time in Syria or someone at the bedside of a dying parent, the act of storytelling itself, the vulnerability that telling the story requires, somehow connects me to the storyteller and reminds me of our shared humanity.

I understand this kind of vulnerability because I told my

own story in my first book, *The Lucky Few.* It was the story of my entrance into motherhood. By sharing my heart and experience with my readers, I allowed them to know me more fully and to feel connected to me in some way. Since *The Lucky Few* was published, literally hundreds of people have asked for my advice about writing a book. I find this a bit hilarious because the truth is that I still barely know how to write a book myself. But here is the best piece of advice I give to all the amazing humans who feel the desire to get their words out there for the world to read: *everyone has a story that should be told and should be heard.*

The first step to telling that story in book form is *words on paper.* You have to get the words on the paper in order to write a book.

Simple enough, right? Well, as a person who is in the act of this step at this very moment, I can tell you that writing a book is more difficult than anything I can put into "words of advice." First of all, writing a book takes time—so very much time. And when life is happening around you, and your youngest is home from school with the pukes or the principal calls from your middle daughter's school to discuss a grit-your-teeth kind of event that happened between your daughter and her peers or your ridiculously adorable son wants nothing more than to play superheroes with you, time is not something that just falls into your lap.

Or when you do find yourself with an hour or two to devote to your writing, you suddenly find you have nothing to say. *Nothing to say!* As though the creative section of your brain is on strike, and the section of your brain where the to-do lists are kept starts screaming at you at the top of its lungs or the portion of your brain called "Amazon shopping" won't shut up and you remember you've been meaning to order that one thing. All of these are real struggles in the life of a writer—or at least in *this* writer's life.

But I've found what causes even more havoc to the art and necessity of sharing one's story is a merciless five-letter word: *d-o-u-b-t*. I am all too familiar with this ruthless little bugger. If you want to find the source of your doubt, all you have to do is take a look at what or whom you're comparing yourself to. I think of comparison and doubt as a sinister pair of playground bullies stomping around, taking the other kids' toys, and trying to ruin recess. In both my writing and my speaking, when I compare my story to my friend's story or to that super-hip blogger's story or to the story of the mom who manages to get it all done in a day or to the story of the successful person who has a lot more resources than I have, I doubt my story, doubt my voice, doubt myself.

Whether or not you ever want to publish your story, my advice to all of us is to stop believing the lies that comparison and doubt love to tell. Instead, believe the truth that your story is important and worth telling simply because *it is yours*. It can be no one else's, and no one can share it like you can—and that is reason enough for you to tell it. You can trust your voice because it is your voice.

Because writing, speaking, and social media make up a large part of my life, you may be tempted to think I have this down—that I no longer have to suck it up and do battle with the mental playground bullies. But that is *not* the case. Doubt and comparison continue to sneak up on me when I write, speak, and even post on Instagram, tempting me to look at what everyone else is doing, leading me to compare my story with others. And there have been too many times when I let doubt creep in and tell me I should not be a person of influence in certain spaces.

I'm not very good at trusting my voice and my influence. That's just the truth. Trusting my voice is so much easier said than done. For example, when I speak at an event, I listen to the other speakers on stage and am convinced they are more articulate or powerful in their message. I watch and listen, wondering how I can be more like them as a speaker. And when I'm working on a writing project, I read a lot and feel discouraged because I will never be able to write like the writers I so admire, or even the ones I don't! I even doubt my place in the social media world. Looking at other influencers' social media posts, I wonder what it would take for my posts to be more like their posts. Honestly? This doubt/comparison dynamic is ugly, and it can easily spiral out of control. This is where I have to push away the obnoxious self-doubt and hold tightly to the truth I know in my heart: *my voice is important because it is my voice.*

That doesn't mean I shouldn't get better at speaking, writing, and social media. There is incredible value when we find mentors within our craft, people from whom we can learn, people who will guide and advise us as we find and use our own voice. It's also okay for me to acknowledge that there will always be speakers and authors I admire who are actually better at their crafts than I am. But I can't let what other people are good at be the standard that sets the value of my role and my story. I can't find my worth by comparing my abilities to the abilities of another. Another person's ability to speak or write does not lessen my ability to speak or write.

When people who are talented share their talents with the world, it does not make me mediocre. Their significance does not make me insignificant. The real kicker here is the fact that when we are doing the thing God places in our path, the thing we are called to, then our talents and efforts and influence become part of a bigger story—part of God's story—and there is no room for doubt or comparison or insignificance in that narrative. That's what allows me to keep pressing forward and to keep telling my story. Once we get a handle on these truths, we can step into the influence we have with confidence.

To help me manage the bullies, I make it a habit to write two things on the top of the notes for every talk I give: "God's story, God's glory!" and "Trust your voice!" I also say these sentences out loud when I sit down to write—before I put a single word on paper. It's key for me to remember how I got to where I am, and that where I am is God's good, good grace over my life. Anything I put my hand to is by God's grace. When I listen to doubt and comparison, it's easy to get all caught up in my own mind and forget why I write or speak the words at all. So I remind myself, *God's story, God's glory.* Whenever doubt tempts me to make it all about me, to focus on myself and my abilities, I look at my sweet little family and I know I could never have made this happen on my own.

As we share our stories and learn from one another, let's remember that one person's story is not better or worse than another's or more worthy of sharing. I understand, though, how someone who is a mom may struggle with this. Whether stay-at-home or working, when she toils away in her little corner of the world, waking up day after day, making oatmeal, going to work, coming home, doing laundry, playing with Legos, making dinner, and then doing the same thing all over again, it can make her think that what other women or moms in the world are doing is more important, and that the work of her hands is not significant enough to share.

I understand this mom because I have been this mom. But let's name this line of thinking for what it is—a lie. The work of a mom is the most significant work I can think of. And her influence is vast. Whether you're a stay-at-home mom or a mom who stands on stages in front of thousands, or you're somewhere in between, your story and your influence are significant because they are yours, and you have the gift and privilege of choosing to own them and then share them with the people in your life.

Because of the writing and speaking I do, I've actually experienced the comparison dynamic from both sides. I compare myself to others, and others compare themselves to me. When people hear our story of adoption and Down syndrome, they often say something like, "Wow! You and your husband are so amazing. Such saints. I could never do what you've done." Okay. This may be true? More accurately, however, it's not!

Even so, I can relate to this feeling that other people give of themselves in a way I can't imagine doing. I've felt the exact same feelings. For example, I was asked to join a Facebook group for people who have adopted kids with Down syndrome.

The person who started the group chose a handful of mamas to be the advice givers and question answerers for other people who join in search of more information about adopting kids with Down syndrome.

In the first post on the Facebook page, the woman who started it asked each of us to share a picture and brief description of our journey. By the time I got around to doing this, four other families had already shared. I sat in astonishment as I read each of their stories.

The first read, "We have five adult homegrown kids, five kiddos adopted from the U.S. foster care system, and four girls with [Down syndrome] adopted from China." Yes, if you did the math correctly, that is fourteen children. *Fourteen.* Four with Down syndrome. *Four.*

The next one read, "We have eight kiddos—three oldest bio daughters, five littles with Down syndrome . . . Our littles are nine, seven, six, five, and three." You read that right—five small children with Down syndrome. Five children between the ages of nine and three, all with Down syndrome. *Five.*

But it doesn't end there, oh no, it does not. The mama who shared right before I did wrote, "We have ten incredible babes this side of heaven and are in the process of adopting our eleventh. One homegrown, five domestic, five China. Our three youngest . . . soon to be four youngest, all have [Down syndrome]." As I write, they now have eleven children. Four of whom have Down syndrome. *Four.*

Whoa! That is actually the word I used at the beginning of my post in which I shared about my apparently tiny family of five. Not five children, but five people—total. And just as people who hear our story approach me and tell me how what we're doing is "so amazing" and how they "could never do it," I look at these families and want to say, "You are so amazing! You are saints! I could never do what you're doing!" And I think all of the above is true because if I were doing what they are doing, then I wouldn't be doing what I need to be doing.

Each and every one of the families in that Facebook group is a book waiting to be written. I have spoken at retreats for adoptive mamas, and when I stand on the stage, having been given the honor of sharing my story, I know I'm sharing in a room full of women who have stories worthy of being shared on a stage. I know there are stories being lived out that would make a much better book than any I could write. But I also know that this doesn't mean my story should not be written. My voice is important and my story is sacred because they are mine, and I have chosen to share them with the world.

This is a truth that is worth repeating: my voice is important and my story is sacred because they are mine. And dear reader, your voice is important and your story is sacred because they are yours.

Look, some of us have much louder voices than others. Sriracha mamas, you know who you are. Some people in this world shout simply for the purpose of shouting. And many people feel overlooked and undervalued simply because their vocal cords don't match the decibel levels of those around them. Any marmalade mamas want to say amen? If you have a loud voice, use it. If you speak in a mere whisper, speak. It doesn't matter how loud your voice is; what matters is that you use it. And when you do, know that your words have power and influence, so be wise and be thoughtful, but own it.

At the same time, remember that speaking and listening are a matched pair—never exercise one without the other. If we believe our words and stories are powerful and we choose to share them within our spheres of influence, then we also have to affirm the power of listening—and diligently practice both. We do not share our stories to make others feel the need to compare their lives to ours, and we do not listen to the stories of others to compare our lives to theirs. We share our stories and listen to the stories of others so we can better understand one another and feel a greater sense of connectedness. When we see how we are connected to others, we can more clearly see the influence we have on the world.

When I think about people who have had great influence, few compare with Mother Teresa. Her influence has spread across the entire world. Movies have been made and books have been written about her life. When she was alive, she was honored with numerous awards, including the Nobel Peace Prize, and in 2016, just nine years after her death, she was canonized as a saint. After winning the Nobel Peace Prize, she was asked by a reporter, "What can we do to promote world peace?" Here's the advice this world-changing saint gave to the rest of us who want to follow in her footsteps: "Go home and love your family."[11] *Boom.*

We don't need to do something on a grand scale in order to have grand influence. What makes our influence grand is simply choosing to step into it. Consider my dear friend Dana, who is a mother of three and a successful business owner who works full-time. Her day-to-day begins with getting up before the sun so she can sit with God for a few moments before her kids wake up. She then goes full speed into mom/boss mode until her head hits the pillow at night. About once a month, she gets her whole family up early on a Saturday morning, packs a bunch of sack lunches, gathers all the gently used clothing they've been collecting, and drives to a section of Los Angeles called Skid Row, where there's a large homeless population. Together with her kids, she distributes lunches and clothes and tells the people with whom she interacts—many of whom she knows well—that they are valuable and loved. She is fully aware that she could do more, that the homeless crisis needs more than sack lunches and clothes, but she is also aware of where God has placed her in this season of life and of the influence she has in those places. Dana has grand influence.

Or consider my friend Olivia. Olivia has two daughters, and her oldest, Sarah, who is twenty-eight, has Down syndrome. Sarah has some serious health issues that require daily attention. So, in addition to being Sarah's mom, Olivia has become an expert in the skills required to tend to Sarah's health needs, and she spends her days as Sarah's full-time caregiver. Olivia reflects Jesus so beautifully. I've never heard her complain about the fact that she gets very little time to herself or that she has had to let go of some of the things in her life she once enjoyed to make space for her role as a caregiver. And when I asked her to be our advocate at Macyn's and August's IEP meetings, she graciously agreed.

During one of our times together in preparation for an IEP meeting, she told me she really enjoyed helping me out because it made her feel useful. I told her from where I sit, I see her using her life in tremendously useful and impactful ways. She has the knowledge and the heart to write books and stand on stages and influence thousands, yet her influence is most powerful because she embraces her role as her daughter's caregiver, offering her daughter a fuller life and giving all who have the honor of watching, a glimpse at the heart of God in the process.

Then there's my friend Christy-Joy, who as a mom of four has a deep desire to empower other moms. She started a movement called "Mom The Day," and she spends countless hours creating events and putting together projects in which she honors all types of moms. I've had numerous conversations with Christy-Joy about what a brilliant concept "Mom The Day" is and how it deserves a huge platform with millions of followers. And yet it hasn't seemed to take off in this way. Not yet, at least. Even so, she remains committed to the cause, knowing it's not the size of the audience that makes it meaningful, but rather the depth and richness of the fruit her work produces that matters most. She knows "Mom The Day" has the potential to positively affect the lives of thousands, even millions, of moms, and she stands fully and boldly in her influence, seeing the impact it has on the lives of those currently within its reach.

These are just a few examples of women I know who are using their influence well, but the truth is, I could go on and on. I could share stories about hundreds of moms I know who have adopted kids from orphanages who would have been forgotten and left to die had they not been adopted. And the grandparents who show up to love on their grandchildren, offering us mamas and papas a much-needed break. Or the single mom who shows up for a job she's not passionate about and then gets home and does dinnertime and bedtime and loves on her kids, day after day, with little or no break. Or the mom who sees that her friend is having a tough day, and so she drops off flowers and offers to watch the kids for a few hours.

In a world where we are encouraged to think the power of our influence hinges on Instagram Likes and YouTube videos going viral, it can be tempting to believe that unless we have a large following or platform, our influence is insignificant. But the truth is, our greatest influence is right where Mother Teresa said it is—in our homes, with the kids we are raising, and in our communities, with the people we're doing life alongside. Our influence is in the places and in the ways we show up.

Once we understand the power of our voice and the impact of our influence, we can truly begin to do the hard work required to make space in this world for the people who tend to be left out. It will require us to scoot over first if we want our kids to be the kind of people who scoot over and make some room for others as well.

So let's do it, friends. Let's step up onto the stages in our lives and with boldness, humility, and vulnerability speak into the microphone and share our stories with the world. Then as boldly and humbly and vulnerably as we spoke, let's hand the mic to someone else and sit and listen as others do the same. We can always leave a seat open for the other. And when we do, we create an opportunity to see the fullness of God by seeing his fullness in the lives of the other—and in so doing, we create a space for everyone to belong.

ACKNOWLEDGMENTS

Gosh! I think this is one of the most difficult parts of the book to write because a few words of gratitude will never do justice when it comes to saying thank you to the people on these pages. And not a single word in this whole book would exist without all of you. But I'll give it my best shot. Here we go, in no particular order.

The Down syndrome community, which I know is literally hundreds of thousands of you—I see you. I see the hard work we are doing together. I'm so thankful to be in this community with every single one of you. For each one of you who shares your stories of hope, unconditional love, and grit with me, I'm grateful and consider it an honor. Thank you for your commitment to shifting the narrative. The world *is* a better place because of it.

More specifically within that community—

- Nancy Littiken—the impact you and Mike have had on the Down syndrome community reaches farther than you can imagine. You are narrative shifters and differences makers, and my role as a mother to children with Down syndrome is more meaningful and impactful because of your example and friendship. Thank you!

- The mamas who share that "Down syndrome gleam" and who have become a safe space for me to run to because you get it—Olivia Hinojosa, Marlena Fletcher, Mercedes Lara, Lyndsey Boulton, Michelle Sullivan, Liz Placta, Lisa Eicher, Lisa Gungor, Mica May, Micha Boyett, Oakley Peterson, Jamie Lim Lee, and Amy Amaradio, to name just a few.

To the educators who have first seen my kids and all their potential and then seen their differences as something to celebrate, learn from, and embrace—please never quit teaching.

To my mentors and friends in the racial reconciliation space—Jamie Lim Lee, Christine Suh, Jasmine Shupper, Tiana Spencer, Christy Joy Meeks, John Williams—thank you for being patient and gracious with me as I learn. Thank you for taking the time to read parts of the book in advance, for speaking truth, and for giving me your input. And John, thank you for meeting up with me over coffee or hummus and helping me get some of these words on paper. I am forever learning from you and always thankful for your wisdom and friendship.

Alison Hooper Keslake, your open heart and flexibility created a stage for our Macyn to dance on—a stage that changed the lives of all of us. Thank you!

To my "amigos para siempre," you have all been a life-giving well of comfort, challenge, and companionship. I consider each of you like family. I thank God for our time together in Monrovia.

Micha Boyett, remember when I handed you thirty to forty thousand words of "word vomit" on paper and then you honestly and kindly coached me and helped me turn it into this book? Thank you for that! Your gift of words is one I'm grateful to glean from.

To my team at Zondervan, thank you for seeing the message of this book as one worth publishing and for taking another chance on me.

To Christine Anderson—who would have guessed that all those years ago when we met in the Newark airport on our way to the Holy Land that we would be working on a book together a few years later. I am so very, very, VERY thankful for your editing genius. Thank you for pushing me to make the words work when they didn't and for hearing my voice and message and making it sing. You are a rock star editor, my friend.

Lisa Jackson! I am forever grateful that you saw a story in me all those years ago, and that you've continued to encourage me to tell it. Also thank you for not letting me quit when I was seriously going to. Seriously.

Mom and Dad—thanks for having me! And thanks for raising me to be the person God made me to be. Your continuous wisdom, love, and unconditional support helped get these words on the pages.

And to all my family—my dedicated and supportive mother-in-love, Jay, and father-in-love, Steve. To my sisters, my ride-or-die—I don't think either of you have a clue how very grateful I am to have you both.

My main guy, Joshua Douglas Avis—you are my compass. Thank you for always bringing me back to the main things, even when I don't want to hear it. Your words of love, grace, and truth are always exactly what I need. Plus, you're the handsomest guy I know and the person I will adventure with for a lifetime. I adore you, babe!

And I thank God for giving me the kids I have. I am a better person because of them, with a greater understanding of the fullness of the goodness of God. They have taught me to see the beauty and worth in every single person I come across. And this, my friends, is a glorious gift!

NOTES

1. Brennan Manning, *The Ragamuffin Gospel* (1990; repr., Colorado Springs: Multnomah, 2015), 145.
2. Heidi Murkoff, *What to Expect the First Year*, 3rd ed. (1989; repr., New York: Workman, 2014).
3. Martin Luther King Jr., *Strength to Love* (1977; repr., Minneapolis: Fortress, 2010), 1–2.
4. Jean Vanier, *Becoming Human* (1998; repr., Toronto, ON: House of Anansi, 2008), 78–79.
5. Quoted in Krista Tippett, *Becoming Wise: An Inquiry into the Mystery and Art of Living* (New York: Penguin, 2016), 85.
6. Quoted in Tippett, *Becoming Wise*, 84.
7. Terry Tempest Williams, "Engagement," *Orion*, July–August 2004, https://orionmagazine.org/article/engagement.
8. "The Sacred Circle," April 2011, www.foreverbecoming.com/2011/04/sacred-circle.html.
9. Vanier, *Becoming Human*, 76.
10. Vanier, *Becoming Human*, 84.
11. Quoted in Tom Rapsas, "Mother Teresa—On Why Loving Your Family Is the Most Important Thing You Can Do," May 2, 2016, *Patheos*, www.patheos.com/blogs/wakeupcall/2016/05/advice-from-mother-teresa-on-making-your-world-a-better-place.

The Lucky Few

Finding God's Best in the Most Unlikely Places

Heather Avis

These are the faces who call me "mom"—the three children who made me a mother.

When I started my journey into parenthood I never thought it would look like this. I never planned on having three adopted children, and I certainly never imagined that two of them would have Down syndrome. But like most of the things God does, once we stepped into the craziness and confusion of the unknown and unplanned, we quickly realized we were indeed among the lucky few.

When my husband and I decided to grow our family ten years ago, we were surprised to find that getting pregnant was not as easy as we had thought it would be. And as we navigated the ups and downs of infertility, God led us down the path of adoption. Of course we would adopt! Not what we had originally planned, but certainly a wonderful option.

But just as we began to get a comfortable grasp on growing our family through adoption, God introduced us to Macyn Hope, a very sick little girl with Down syndrome who desperately needed a family. As we continued to follow God's calling, first with Macyn and later with Truly and then August, we found ourselves further and further from the comfortable paths we thought our lives would take and instead moving down some very scary and often painful roads.

Even though at times God's plan seemed terrifying and even downright foolish, little could we have known how much goodness, blessing, and joy would flow out of loving these three little people God has put into our lives. No, it hasn't been easy—not the open-heart surgeries, the challenges of raising two children with Down syndrome, the complexities of dealing with birth families, or the struggles with the public education system. But through it all, every new and uncomfortable situation has only proven to be another chance to see how very good God's plan is for our lives and how downright lucky we are to be able to live it out.

It's only the lucky few who recognize that the most beautiful things in this life are often found in the differences. What some would see as misfortune, I've learned to see as nothing more than pure luck.